I0818370

BLACK

FISH

BLACK

how to fish, and stories of
the wata, kin & community

SPEECH DEBELLE

FISH

Black Fish
Speech Debelle

This edition first published in the UK and USA in 2026 by
Watkins, an imprint of Watkins Media Limited
Unit 11, Shepperton House
89-93 Shepperton Road
London N1 3DF

enquiries@watkinspublishing.com

Commissioning Editor: Ella Chappell
Head of Design: Karen Smith
Designed by Ana Pryor
Typeset by Steve Williamson
Production: Uzma Taj

10 9 8 7 6 5 4 3 2 1

Printed and bound by CPI Group (UK) Ltd, Croydon, CR0 4YY

The manufacturer's authorised representative in the EU for product safety is:
eucomply OÜ - Pärnu mnt 139b-14, 11317 Tallinn, Estonia,
hello@eucompliancepartner.com, www.eucompliancepartner.com

A CIP record for this book is available from the British Library

ISBN: 978-1-83681-026-1 (Hardback)
ISBN: 978-1-83681-027-8 (eBook)

www.watkinspublishing.com

CONTENTS

SPEECH DEBELLE, AGE 32
Photography taken by Ty Faruki 2015

The First Time I Fished

The first time I fished, I was 33. I like to imagine I was drawn to some kind of secret duality in the two repeating numbers, reminding me of two soldiers standing in arms facing the same direction, or two Notting Hill Carnival parade dancers connected to each other, locked into the rhythm and whine perfectly. A natural inclination to register patterns. A need to make sense of things.

Before then, or more specifically, at the age of 30, I did not know how to live in my own body. I'm still learning how. How to be in the present, without the anxiety of future social engagements and conversations that want to pull from a body still in its thawing process. Not yet knowing how to regulate my emotions, hitting seven, on the 0 – 10 internal meter, before I've even said a word. Leaving anyone clearly unaware by my stoic disposition of the implosion taking place. But this has been my work. If there were a karmic agreement I made before entering this life, I get the sneaking suspicion this work of being present was a key part of negotiations.

Over time I'm becoming more comfortable with how uncomfortable being open and in the present feels. No longer so anxious and on 10mg of Sertraline to temper a nervous system overly obsessed with what *could* happen, and without the need for continuous avoidance tools like Jameson Whiskey to numb the pain of what *has* happened.

Many days you can often catch me on the shoreline of the UK with two fishing rods facing the sky, for a time, concerned only with how high or low the sun is on the horizon. Or giving a nod of attention to the distance of the incoming tide and wondering whether I should move backward away from it now or give it another 30 minutes or so before re-shuffling my fishing gear. As though time is being represented by the movement of nature.

Fishing is one of the mechanisms I've discovered that not only grounds and centres me but reminds me of my ancestral connection to the wata and the healing it offers.

I'm Black, I'm queer and my visual for this is spray-painted like street art on a British institutional building in the City of London. It's in your face and it's a disruption of the "norm". Interrupting spaces not designed for those that look like me comes with the territory, and the world of fishing is no different. The angling [to fish with a rod and line] world has been co-opted by humans who present as opposite to me as it can get. My partner (also Black and queer) and I have walked into tackle shops, and I swear to you, we've heard the cowboy music play as we walk in and the shop doors swing shut slowly behind us. Every white man who happens to be in that tackle shop at the time spins his head like Supa D teasing the drop of that remix we've only heard on the Soundcloud mix and are now hearing live and direct in the club. The person behind the till, we can only guess, assumes we are lost and looking for directions. Like we can't find the beach – as though we've been transported to a time before smartphones. "Hi, where are your two-hook flapper rigs please," we query as he points us in the direction of the stand lined with plastic protected fishing rigs, questioning his own assumptions. But what is an absolute and without prejudice, is that the coastline belongs to us all. So, we get the rigs we need and we keep moving. Sometimes existing is an act of rebellion itself.

Why I chose fishing as a soul that needed saving is not much different to why most people have chosen it, is my guess. It's not that strange, when you one day have a moment of clarity that comes with an extra shot of coffee out of nowhere.

- I needed a new hobby that took me away from being in a system that wants me to be constantly productive for reasons that are not so high on my list of priorities anymore – or ever.
- I needed some calm and healing – the kind you get from being in front of a body of wata.
- I needed to feel like I was learning something fresh, to spark that childlike excitement you get from the new and unknown.
- I needed that dopamine, serotonin and oxytocin coursing through my body the way it should, when the drugs in major cities was filled with toxins and the come down was never worth the going up.
- I needed some *me*-time, and I didn't mind sharing that me-time with others who know they need the same.

The routes and journeys of why fishing has sparked our interest may be different for each of us, but when you add it up, you can see how we may have got here. And what an honour to have the journeys we've had and arrive at a place that feels like our own decision. That me time.

So, on my 33rd birthday I booked my first fishing lesson with an Englishman I found through a vague online search, whose name I can't remember. He taught lessons in his spare time for a little extra money, and it gave him another reason to fish, something he doesn't get do as much as he used to. I sat next to him on a bank of a lake, on those camping chairs with the holder for your drink – which you always notice, whether you have a drink to put in it or not – as he walked me through the sequence. He never really made eye contact, which I didn't mind at all. We spent most of the time sitting and watching the tip of the rod for some "action" and talking about the different fish in the lake. There was a lot of information on the set up of the rod, the bait we were using and the fish species that I had no way of processing and truly digesting at the time, but I enjoyed the flood of knowledge I was receiving nonetheless, so I let him rip. The feeling of not knowing what I was doing, while attempting to do it, tickled me. We discussed why fishing just "isn't what it used to be" because of trawlers and bureaucracy and "too many people everywhere", which type people he didn't say, and I didn't ask. We discussed why getting older seemed to be a contract he did not remember signing, and I could imagine the invisible ink was chemically reacting and revealing itself to him incrementally as he spoke. I nodded and smiled, and let what was meant for me in. Still, we made very little eye contact, which I still didn't mind. We were connecting on this bank in front of the wata while we fished.

He mentioned working for a local council when he had lived in London before moving just a little out of the city. At the time, I had also just moved out of London, a little outside of the city. I asked him which council, because my mum also worked for a council and her role sounded vaguely similar to his – as much as I ever knew truly what she did. (Sidebar – did you ever call your mum at work to ask for £5 or to let you go out with friends that day or just to find out what was for dinner, like she wasn't at work with *actual* work to be getting on with?) Alas, his answer shocked me, and for the first time that day, we made eye contact. This man, a man I'd never met before but found online for a good price and who was free that day – called John or maybe not – had worked in the same council as my mum, at the same time. I told him her name, and he described her as anyone would: "A short lady, cute?" Yes!

We have these random connections of events called coincidences that seem to be divinely orchestrated and mathematically perfect. We get nudges from some higher power to let us know, like seeing 11:11 every time we pick up the phone or the number 4 daily for a week. It's like something or someone is saying, "I see you, keep going".

Look, fishing is fishing, it's not winning the lottery. I'm not saying you pick up a rod at your local corner shop and your life instantly changes. But it is one of the things you may do that makes you feel better the more you do it. And over time, it may be part of a saving grace, and if so, you'll get those nudges.

Here's what I now believe to be true about me and fishing. My need to find myself and be back in my body led me to it. Fishing then led me to other new passions like catch-and-cook videos, foraging and survival techniques. My passions were contrasting themes about how to survive in this world. They were telling me to save my own life, as though I was walking through a succession of doors while the universe whispered "warmer, warmer, warmer".

Before I fished, I searched for relationships and activities that recreated a lack of safety, as my body and nervous system had come to understand this "posed for what may come next" setting as its norm. Instead of the "peace and non-reciprocal care" setting we should also be able lean into. Instead of craving what kept me on the edge of my consciousness, I started to crave stillness. Just to turn off the pretence of high function for a while and release my strained back and taut shoulders, for a few hours a day.

I've fallen in love with this thing called fishing and now I dream of it most days.

We Are Black Fish

This book began its life in 2022 when I approached an agency about a Tarot deck I had made with an old friend. The deck features artwork inspired by the Rider Waite classic but using the colours of the chakras and chosen lyrics from my previous four albums to create its own divination. Although they did not publish and distribute the cards, they were polite about their non commitment. Those kinds of "no's" that are kneaded for the right amount of time and laid on the dinner table well enough that you still feel nourished after hearing them. The agency's owner wanted to know if I had considered writing a book. Yes, was the short answer. As an rapper and poet, I had written words all my life. I'd even had meetings over the years with book publishers. But my ideas had got responses like "It just doesn't fit in anywhere specifically". Writing about one subject that fits in one section of a book shop was just not something I was innately able to do. Life is a tangled weave of interconnected parts and … I'm complex, bruv!

Over the next two years we kept in touch and, in one of our catch ups, we discussed the newly formed fishing community my partner and I set up – We Are Black Fish – as well as me having been an angler for some years now. I told stories of catching, nearly catching and how I cook the catch; how, on paper, the community is a fishing club, but looking more closely, it's a mechanism for joy centring black, global majority and queer people and their intersection on the path back to wata, which we have been systematically separated from.

How what we do when we meet at the coastline to learn to fish together each month is an act of ritual. We practise tying a blood knot while we stand in a group and use our hands to weave the knots in the desired direction. Other people's hands that look just like ours help our hands form the correct placements, which are like ignition sparks for memories of our loved ones teaching us to tie shoelaces. Just using our hands again reminds us to be present in our bodies, something that we don't get to do enough.

By the end of that catch up, the owner and her very new and bright-eyed trainee had heard something that meant something to them too.

With their help we formed this idea of questioning why someone like me, and the people that return each month to the group, chose this thing we call fishing. The book had taken first form.

The title was the easiest part to be cemented and was present from the beginning. It was there waiting for me before I even fished. Have you seen the 2013 documentary "Black Fish"? You must have. It's in, or should be in, every top ten greatest documentary lists. Who knew a film about an orca named Tilikum captured in 1983 and kept in SeaWorld to entertain until its death 2017 would change my life this way. If you've seen it, I'm sure you recognise the impact, but let me explain.

The plight of these orcas – majestic creatures, captured and used as tools for financial gain and treated as commodities – felt like a very, very familiar story. While watching this powerful documentary I couldn't help but draw parallels to what people have, and still do, experience.

Captivity and Exploitation

The documentary begins with former SeaWorld employees speaking about what it was like to "work" with the orcas. They speak of how drawn they were to spend time with these mammals, recounting childhood memories of visiting SeaWorld that stuck with them – that feeling we all get when we are introduced to something that calls to us and we see what our future could look like. In their innocence and privilege, to be with the creatures, to love them and bond with them, meant accepting the valiant challenge of training them to perform. Within the first five minutes of the film, we are shown how the structures of whiteness operate in deluding those who most benefit from it into believing exploitation is a way of life. The soft background music plays in chords of major 6th, so we feel the warmth watching these loving retellings. But what is being said? What has actually been done?

The documentary shares the story of how this particular orca named Tilikum, was captured, stolen and transported to this pool for entertainment by skirting the lines of legality. Men on huge boats were sent to collect at least one orca from a family of orcas in the North Atlantic Ocean near Iceland. They were paid well and they were prepared with ammunition and powerful engines. Speed boats threw bombs into the water to scare and force the orcas in the desired direction making them easier to separate. In the chaos they were able to capture the "little ones" as they were instructed to, which were easier on the pocket to transport and would live longer so they could get more years of entertainment out of them. Tilikum was moved across the oceans into an unknown place on the other side of the world. Sounds familiar, right?

The Emotional Impact on the Capturers

I was unexpectedly moved by the retelling of Tilikum's theft from his natural life by one of the hired capturers who expressed profound guilt and shame years later. It made me think about how these structures protect those that benefit from them from the shock and horror they may feel if they were able to truly see the consequences of their actions, or inactions that keep them in the comfort of the colonial structure. Like how one can watch the devastation being brought against people in Palestine or the Congo and feel deep empathy, as they scroll through countless videos on social media. But that doesn't mean one is able to retrace the steps to what protects and provides *their* own sense of freedom, and how it is drawn like blood from the people they are watching. Keeping it as a *they* problem, over there.

Tilikum's capturer paused in his retelling and welled up, as the guilt hit his chest, tightening the muscles in his neck, stopping the words from being able to escape. An impact of this kind transcends time. Dr Joy DeGruy has a brilliant lecture called "Post Traumatic Slave Syndrome" in which she astutely and evidentially connects the physiological effects of the African Slave Trade to not just the descendants of those who were enslaved, but also the descendants of those who benefited.

Physical Trauma

While Tilikum was being kept in essentially a bathtub compared to its size and the distance it should travel in an average day, its confinement manifested in the changing of its physical form. Tilikum's fin bent over like it was collapsing, like it was bearing a weight. A transmutation from the years spent unable to move in the way its elegant body was designed to do. I think this shows up for us people too. Even in small ways, like being in a land that doesn't provide enough sunlight for melanin rich bodies, resulting in a lack of Vitamin D being absorbed and making them more prone to deficiency. Yet being expected to perform as normal, not to make a fuss. The scientists on both sides of the documentaries argued about the reasons for the collapsed fin. Studies were written. Many court dates were attended. But at the time of the film's release in 2013, Tilikum was still at SeaWorld.

Spiritual Significance

A quote from the documentary imprinted on me: "First Nations called them black fish, an animal with great spiritual power and not to be meddled with."

Just as I see reflections in the treatment of the orcas featured in the documentary, I hear the words of the indigenous people who warn of what this treatment could mean. Just as we cut down the trees and cause more floods, how we treat the people and the animals will also be felt. With orcas' high intelligence and spiritual power, are we surprised at the rise of attacks on boats primarily in the Iberian Peninsula, the exact sea bordering Portugal, a land known as the birthplace of the African Slave Trade? Am I making a wide connection here? Yes. But it *is* all connected. It *is* that deep.

Wata

We may be suffering from spiritual amnesia and have forgotten that wata itself is a form of memory that carries stories in it, as well as people across it. We forget it's even there most of the time, just like forgetting parts of ourselves. Each time we interact with it, we're adding to this memory and sparking our own, which may be a reason we are so drawn to it when we need it. In all its forms, it seems to answer our calls to understand ourselves more.

In David Attenborough's film *Ocean*, he says "Living for nearly a hundred years on this planet, I now understand that the most important place on Earth is not on land, but at sea, for if we save the sea, we save our world. After a lifetime of filming our planet, I'm sure that nothing is more important."

Has our "Uncle David"– as I like to call him – come to know first-hand *some* of what indigenous communities across the planet have been trying to tell us? That our respect for this great resource is directly connected to our own humanity. But as sincere as the sentiment is, do we need to save the planet? Or are we in fact what needs saving from this cycles of destroy, save, repeat?

I should say, there is a reason I've been (and will be) sometimes spelling water as "wata". I need there to be a separation between the Oxford Dictionary meaning of the word, and the spiritually and emotional value I am adding to its presence and form. To call it "water" in the only language I can speak, feels too sterile in evoking the latter – too small, and inconsequential when speaking of its importance to us. As though it's made up of only separate parts of our lives; droplets that come out of taps, fall randomly from the skies or live at our coastlines getting on with whatever it is meant to be getting on with. But "wata" – the way it feels escaping the mouth – is more like a prayer. It's like the one who loves you saying your name during an interaction that makes you turn to them, as though hearing your name is a reminder that you are you. It's more like a channelling of that flow running through us. When it's just two Black bodies in a sea of otherness, who have never met before. Who share a look that says

– without words and just the slightest of postulation – we have felt, heard and seen in our lives and in our ancestral DNA a subjugation that is undeserving, but has so far not been powerful enough to dampen our currents and waves. More like a verb, something sentiment, alive and constantly in motion.

Researchers have identified traces of what they believe is the earliest known prehistoric ancestor of humans – a microscopic, bag-like sea creature, which lived about 540 million years ago.*

Imagine us, blobs that grew limbs after the tide left us exposed on the land and it only made sense to go ahead and grow a backbone. Nearly impossible to believe when we look around and see what we call "human" now. We've all heard that the human body is made up of around 70 per cent water or that the amniotic fluid we gestate in for nine months mirrors the salinity of seawater, which surely indicates our lives are just a dress rehearsal, a lifetime spent trying to return to the wata and be more *like the wata.* It has always been our first home, even in the body we chose as our entry point to experience this life.

I spoke to Sanjeev Gupta, the geologist attributed for discovering the catastrophic flood over 400,000 years ago, which created the English Channel that now separates England and France. When I asked him about our ancient relationship with the ocean, he says "water was present right from the early stages of life on earth, so really, right at the beginning of earth, there was water. Deep in the oceans there are areas where hot fluids rise up from deep underneath the earth, carrying nutrients. It's theorised that microbes (us) may have generated by using those minerals to develop."

But even though we can point to the wata being our likely origin, there's only so much we can truly know, as the depth of the ocean itself holds the greatest stories from us. Sanjeev and I spoke about his current work with NASA's Mars 2020 rover mission named Perseverance. The rover searches the fiery planet for signs of early life through collected samples in one of the planet's river deltas, to better

---

* https://www.cam.ac.uk/research/news/bag-like-sea-creature-was-humans-oldest-known-ancestor

understand its past geology and water interaction. He muses "And to be honest, you know, we know more about the surface of Mars now than we do about under the ocean."

JUST A DROP IN THE OCEAN – TRAUMA AND BAPTISM

But what are we doing to the wata?

We've seen in our lifetimes how the power of wata will move and reshape all in its path. Take the Indian Ocean earthquake and subsequent tsunami of December 26, 2004. In the space of minutes, an estimated 227,898 people across 14 countries died, a number that shakes us all to the core. We also watched as the levees built to withstand and protect the people in New Orleans were pushed aside with an ease more powerful than humans can comprehend as the wata rushed into mostly the lower ninth ward, an area of predominantly Black and poor white residents, causing mass deaths during hurricane Katrina in 2005.

These moments are not just a reflection of how wata takes us back to it when it is pushed, but also the economic disruption of the "thirsty" systems that take from it and leave the effects to be felt by people they consider less important. This is known by the term *environmental racism*. Where wata should be a universal source of joy, access to it is deeply unequal. For marginalized communities, frolicking in it, whether through swimming, fishing or bathing, is disrupted.

The oceans and seafloors are holding the stories empires have tried to erase. The only true border in our oceans is its depth, which holds these stories tightly. We can only go so far down before the pressure created by its vastness is too much for our bodies or current technology to withstand. We know that many of us have been shipped like packages across this space. Today, I can type my name into the the Legacies of British Slavery Database* and see the origins of my surname from a slave owner in Saint Elizabeth, a parish in Jamaica that was awarded £117 in 1805 for the release of 27 members of my direct lineages. Before then it's impossible to know who exactly my earlier ancestors were, but my direct descendants arrived most likely from the shores of West Africa. My kin have crossed many watas for me to be here.

A scene in the 1997 film *Amistad* depicting the Spanish slave ship *La Amistad* in 1839, and the subsequent revolt, is imprinted in my mind. It may even be imprinted on my ancestral DNA because I *felt* it. It's the scene where the ship is making its treacherous crossing of the Atlantic Ocean. Bodies are being tied to huge rocks and thrown overboard – for being too sick, too old or just creating too much weight to make the passage financially viable. A mother holding her infant sits on the edge of the ship and before anyone gets the chance to see, for reasons they'll figure out quickly, she tips backward and overboard. She chooses death as an act of freedom and the wata as her and her child's final resting place, as their "baptism" from this trauma. Although it's just a scene from a movie, there is evidence to show it's likely a quarter of the people stolen went overboard, a portion of those likely by choice.

Now here's why this scene comes back to me so often. Whenever I'm on holiday, I absolutely book a diving session. I love the magic of

* https://www.ucl.ac.uk/social-historical-sciences/history/research/research-projects-and-centres/centre-study-legacies-british-slavery-cslbs/lbs-database

breathing underwater (again, maybe) and moving with an agility that only the wata provides. When the boat has powered through the waves to be level with the wreck, monument or reef the captain so chooses, we do the diving ritual of sitting on the edge of the boat, backs facing the wata, tank full of oxygen, and then tip ourselves backward on that short freefall before our bodies make impact. But this is a joy for me. It's complex to hold both expressions in our lived experience and in our ancestral memories – the trauma and the baptism.

One of my earliest memories of seeing the elders in my community dancing and joyful together was in a front room in south London in the mid to late 80s. This would have been pre-organised by moving the furniture from the living room into another room that living room furniture did not normally reside, creating space for bodies to move freely while holding paper plates of good food gracefully around each other. They made way for the speakers that pumped both resonant bass and the top notes that carried the words of the song's chorus that everyone joined in. The reason for this all-night, hands-up, sing along of a celebration? A child's christening. The infant was held by a pastor and its forehead was sprinkled with some droplets of holy water, thus welcoming them into a Christian life. All of this, the moving, the cooking, the inviting, the enjoyment, was to celebrate this wata ritual.

In the rivers and lakes around the globe, people still use bodies of wata for bathing. Children are held upright by their mothers while a soapy cloth is used to completely cover their skin from top to tail, and then they are encouraged to dip under the wata to wash away the day.

In Japan, the fishermen whisper *Ebisu*, invoking the god of fishermen and abundance, as gratitude before casting their nets. This fishing deity holds the power of wealth and good fortune, and honouring it is a way of asking to be received and returned to land safely.

In the Yoruba tradition, Yemoja is the goddess of the oceans and rivers. Amber C Snider writes in her piece "Learning to Surrender: The Sacred Lessons of Yemayá", in *The Afro-Caribbean Religions of Santería*, "As one of the oldest and widely known orishas she is known for her nurturing love, emotional healing, help with fertility and protective energies. Wherever there is water, there is Yemayá".

This wata, in all its forms, run through and over our bodies in the same way that it does as the veins of this planet, through and around land masses. In a world where truth is searched for online and returned with a flood of maybes and debates that we try to rely on, wata remains the original teacher: the eloquent master of ceremonies; the first mother and doula; the baptism and the trauma: the keeper of stories, older than the vertebrae that make up our bones.

Which Wata Calls to You To Fish?

Different wata demand different strategies and gear from us to fish them. Using a conventional rod and reel method, we'll look at what's used and how to use them throughout this book. But each of these bodies of wata also has a spiritual meaning. They speak to different parts of our own make up. Making the connection between what part of you they speak to most can help on this journey of learning the art of fishing as an act of coming home to oneself.

There are many types of bodies of wata on our planet, but this book will explore the four most common, with a focus on one – the beach, and fishing done here, which is commonly known as coastal or sea fishing.

Rivers and Streams

For millennia these bodies of wata have been used as a map and direction to follow from one area to another – for example, early African civilizations followed the River Nile north from the sub-Sahara, using it as a pathway to find new lands and resources for living. Wata from higher ground floods down often through rocks, filtering it to become fresh spring wata as it makes its way back to the sea or a large lake. It is a body of wata that is constantly on the move.

Fishing here is about having the least amount of gear possible. It demands that we're adaptable to change and stay curious about its movement. Fish species like trout, salmon, bass, catfish and pike move through these requiring quick fishing action with lures to entice them.

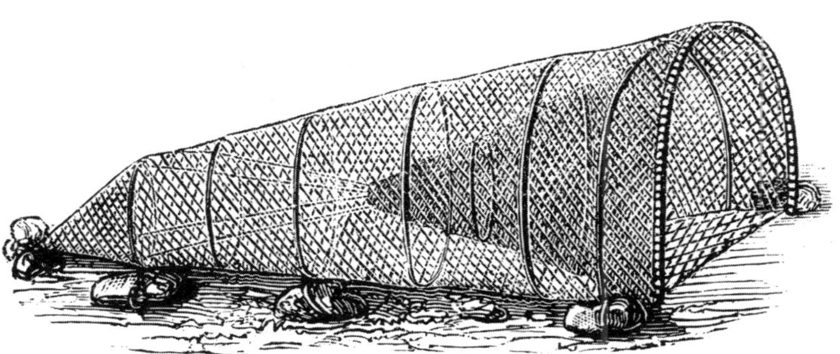

These fish are strong, swimming against currents. They give us a high-adrenaline and fun fishing session.

These bodies of wata represent old and new ideas, like a conversation with a stranger in passing that sticks with you for a lifetime. To fish in a river or stream you need to be firmly connected to the ground with a good grip, even if standing in it.

Lakes, Canals and Ponds

These bodies of wata have an introspective and reflective stillness about them, regardless of their depth. People fish here using gear that is solid and move quietly while doing so, so the species that live here are not spooked. Fish like carp, panfish (bluegill, crappie) and walleye call these bodies of wata home.

There's patience in all fishing, but there's a particular need for stillness here, making the lakes and ponds nature's mirror, reflecting everything back at us as it gets the chance to. Lakes, canals and ponds can be man-made and filled with fish specifically for fishing, but they also grow naturally over time as the wata fills the basin. They have taken a long time to become as still as they are.

Fishing here is a form of deep meditation allowing us to sit with our thoughts. It's no surprise you rarely see a group of people fishing this way – mostly one person alone, as still as a monk in training.

The Open Ocean or Deep Sea

This body of wata covers over 70 per cent of the planet and provides half the oxygen we breathe. It's as though when it released wata onto the land, spilling us out too, it knew we would still need it.

Fishing in these, has been a way of feeding communities for a long time. To fish in deep and open wata is tough and life-risking work. Fishermen head out at night and must learn to read the mood the ocean is in: how the sky is an indication for tomorrow's swell; how the moon pulls her; and the tide timings that must be considered. This kind of fishing for food requires great understanding from watching and listening.

Anglers who are fishing for sport hire charter boats to take them further out to sea and into the ocean to access larger numbers of fish in huge shoals and much larger species. Such fishing requires heavy gear like the strongest of fishing lines (100+ pound) or wire leaders to withstand the sharp teeth and strength of species like tuna, grouper and sharks.

The open and deep wata represents our history of migration and is the keeper of our travelling stories. What has fallen to the seafloor will remain there, archived in the cool, dark gestating ocean floor. Fishing here, there's a requirement to recognise its power, and perhaps our own.

The Wata of the Seashore or Beaches

These are those where we can walk up the edge face to face as they ebb and flow back and forth. The waves and currents of the sea over time have created the mounds of sand and shingle we sunbathe on and use to firmly anchor our fishing tripods upon.

Using beach rods that are longer and allow us to cast further past the shore's breaking waterline, we're able to get a very varied catch from land – not only fish but crustaceans like crab and mussels, prawns and squid live here. Fresh bait cut into strips, worms dug up from the sand or crustaceans collected at low tide are used to draw in a fish, curious about what's on the end of our hook.

Fishing here, we're encouraged to release, as we let what needs to be taken away go and become diluted in the vastness. The wata will take your secrets, hopes and prayers and make you feel much lighter than you felt before, as the waves return methodically, ready to do the work again.

THE PREPARATION

"Today's class is tomorrow's visit."

What Is Fishing?

We should start with the obvious, right? Fishing is an art, simple and elegant in its presentation and executed well by learning how to use our tools and adapting those learned techniques to the environment we're in. Fishing can be simplified in to four things:

1. Wata – whether that be a river, a lake, an estuary, a beach, or an ocean

2. Tools – fishing gear like a rod and reel or even simply some string tied to a hook and a long stick

3. Patience – being willing to put in the hours of watching and waiting; watching while you take in the data and waiting for the bite that we respond to.

4. Fish – whether for food or for a sport hobby.

This breaks it down to the bare bones of the thing – the online recipe that makes exactly six portions if cooked following the right temperature and timings. Then once you've made it enough times, you can play with the recipe.

The Origins of Fishing

It's difficult to pinpoint when fishing started for us as a species. But we can be sure it began with a bellyful of hunger and hope.

The oldest fishing hooks were found in Sakitari Cave, Okinawa, Japan and are dated to be around 23,000 years old, as cited in the Guardian: "Humans are believed to have moved offshore to Okinawa and its sister islands about 50,000 years ago, but much of the history of their adaptation to life there and the evolution of maritime technology is still unknown".* Another source mentions even older evidence: "That these types of fish [tuna, sharks and rays] were being routinely

* https://www.theguardian.com/world/2016/sep/18/worlds-oldest-fish-hooks-okinawa-japan-sakitari-cave

caught 40,000 years ago is extraordinary", says Sue O'Connor from the Australian National University in Canberra. "It requires complex technology and shows that early modern humans in Southeast Asia had amazingly advanced maritime skills." Far older fish bones have been found at sites in southern Africa – those at the Blombos Cave in South Africa, for example, date from 140,000–50,000 years ago.*

There are symbols left in the art on ancient Egyptian tombs dating back 12,000 years, depicting fishing nets, spears and woven traps. And early Maori hooks carved out of whale bones have been discovered, along with the first kind of fishing lures, shaped to mimic fish made from wood and stone, which are styled the same way today.

The difference is, we have a fishing crisis, as humans live longer and there are simply more of us consuming fish. We now have a worldwide global economy where fish isn't just eaten from what we're able to catch, but is offered in every restaurant, supermarket and village market across the planet simultaneously. There are huge commercial fishing operations that collect tons of fish, pushing far beyond my understanding of weight and numbers. Hundreds of thousands of tons are collected each day. I have no reference point for what looks like such astronomical amounts. According to the Food and Agricultural Organisation, an estimated 61.8 million people are engaged in fishing as full-time, part-time, occasional or unspecified workers in the primary sector of commercial fisheries and aquaculture.†

The kind of fishing done now for our daily consumption is diverse, as we are able to access more of the ocean. From the huge trawlers that supply the supermarkets we use when we're musing on what to eat for dinner on the way home, to local fisherman who use nets and traps to catch substantial but humble amounts, to individuals who spearfish each morning for enough fish to hang on the winding beach tree to sell to passers-by.

---

* https://www.historyofinformation.com/detail.php?id=4947

† https://openknowledge.fao.org/server/api/core/bitstreams/66538eba-9c85-4504-8438-c1cf0a0a3903/content/sofia/2024/fisheries-aquaculture-employment.html#:~:text=Employment%20in%20the%20primary%20sector,Europe%20(both%200.1%20percent).

And it's not just fish species that are being collected. It won't be uncommon for us to cast out our lines and reel in a crab or a squid. There are traps and lures designed specifically to catch them, but a hook with some bait can get you just about anything in sea – a reminder that we can't see what's happening on the other end of the line and just how truly diverse salt wata is.

But despite the vast oceans encompassing 70 per cent of the planet, fish species are still under threat. Convenience has caused a complicity. The magic itself of having easy access to fish has become a blindness to the damage being caused.

As we've moved from fishing strictly as a hunting and gathering activity into trawling and farming fish for convenience, we have also turned fishing into a sport, which has grown over the last few decades. There are many tournaments and competitions for landing the biggest weights and sizes, and social media accounts in the millions of people wanting to know the best way to wrap a squid bait or get a first-hand account of what it's like to fish in Florida or Japan. Across the world, we're bonding in this love of the art of fishing. Somewhere in the middle between the chaos and the calm of regulation lies sustainability and a way of providing peace and healing as a pastime. The angler is emerging as a natural custodian, with a direct insight into how the wata is responding to us. Hook and line fishing is how we started all those years ago and taking this up as a hobby, food source, and mechanism for connection now is, in a way, coming full circle.

This thing we call fishing is coded in our DNA, even if not as obvious as mobile phones will show the structural change in our postures in the next century. It is there. A form of hunting, the uniqueness of fishing is in the fact it is mostly done without having eyes on what you're trying to catch. It relies heavily on reading the elements around you. We can rent a boat or a spot on a boat that even comes with the gear for the day. The skipper will be using a sonar that maps out the underwater topography showing us the wrecks fish are drawn to and live in. But even with high tech tools like this, dropping our rods over the edge of the boat and sending out lines and hooks into the deep, we cannot be sure of what's going on down there. But each time we'll learn a little more.

Seabirds like the gannet plunge down to the surface in large groups breaking the point air meets wata with their beaks to hunt the shoals of fish just metres from the edge of the shoreline. This kind of blessing, when we're in the right place at the right time, means we can grab some mackerel, bass or sabiki feathers which embellish each hook with shiny or glow-in-the-dark adornments to look as dazzling as possible. We cast them out into the beautiful chaos of nature's order and then, just like that, the shoal of fish and the gannets move on. We can't be sure of how long they intended to stay, but each time we learn a little more.

We use tide times, guides to show when there will be the most movement in the wata and therefore more fish activity. Or check the wind speed and direction to indicate when predator fish are likely to be closer to shore as they track smaller fish being pushed around in the swell. The wind direction (S, E, N, W) is also an indicator of wata pressure. South and West being considered the best as an indication of falling air pressure and warmer wata activating fish. We have lures specially designed to imitate smaller fish as we stand on rocks or jetties and cast them out, then retrieve quickly so they move like fish darting, until boom – a strike from something big from below. The heart beating moment of a bite. But then, the fish unhooks itself by thrashing left and right, just as we're exclaim excitedly, "Fish on!" to whoever receives the message, in three octaves higher than our normal speaking voice. But that's why it's called fishing and not catching, teaching us in real time that we can only respect the power of how the wata moves and what is alive within in it. We're asking permission with our rod and gear in hand, like some kind of Mayan ritual as we stand in front of this God of wata ready to sacrifice any parts of our gear the rocks or waves feel hungry enough to swallow that day. The techniques and tools have evolved for many of us. But try and always keep in mind the basics of what fishing is and keep investigating why you're drawn to this. Like an affirmation leaving your chest…

wata, tools, patience, fish.

In the next section we'll get into the list of gear you'll need and use for angling, with a focus on saltwater fishing (coast, beach, deep sea). But try to consider even before you begin this fishing journey: *What do I want this to be? Is it for food or for fun, a meditation or creating a community? Or an act of rebellion and/or joy? Or all the above?*

The Gear

Fishing Rods

A rod is essentially the long shaft made from fiberglass, graphite or carbon that extends your line and hooks out into the wata. It's the conductor of the orchestra that brings it all together.

Spinning Rods

These are 10–15ft (3–4.5m) rods used for getting bait out to a further distance when saltwater fishing. If you imagine yourself standing at a shoreline, you'll see you want this longer rod to get that bait as far out as possible. The tip of the rod will be the thinnest section to create a flick-like motion when you cast that gives you more distance. Personally, I like using an ultra-light spinning rod. The day after a long fishing session if I'm not using something light, I feel the strain from casting out and retrieving, akin to that post-gym fatigue I couldn't tell was building up at the time.

Casting Rods

These are normally used with a bait casting reel to match. Typically used when holding over the side of a boat or a pier for larger species in deeper wata, they are designed to be firmer and stronger with not as much give to create the flicking action like a spinning rod.

Lure Rods

These are used when fishing with artificial lures that mimic the movement of small prey fish. Usually 9 – 11ft. You cast out the lure and retrieve it in different styles, which we'll look into with more detail in the Fishing Chapter. Because of this constant movement, lure rods are shorter and lighter (although still strong because of the greater amount of bend they allow before breaking) but with the same thin tip as a spinning rod for the flick action. They are used on all bodies of wata.

Feeder and Float Rods

These are most commonly used in canals and fishing lakes. The feeder rod is usually 10–16ft (3–5m) with a sensitive tip but solid and strong throughout its length. There's not much bend, if any, in these rods. The bait is placed in a cage connected to the line and dropped to bottom.

A float rod is like a feeder rod in that it is used in the same kind of wata's, but it is designed to be used with a float that holds the bait on the hook at a desired length *in* the wata column instead of on the bottom. Because of this, it is lighter, so it is more comfortable if you want to hold the rod rather than set it down while waiting for a bite.

Fishing Reels

The reel is the mechanical heart of the whole set up. It pumps the line through your rod that holds the hooks or lure on the other end. It controls the releasing and retrieving of your line and creates the tension to manage the fish when caught. Reels all have spools that hold the line, a brake mechanism for slower or faster retrieval and a handle to manually wind the line in, which can be swapped easily from one side to another, for left or right-handed use. Although they come in many sizes, the following are the two most-used reels.

Spinning Reels

These are the most common types of reel and the easiest to use. A spinning reel is a great starting place as you can easily buy a spinning rod and reel combo online or at tackle shops. The fishing line is held on the spool of the reel and controlled by the bail arm, which allows the line to come out when open and stops it from being let out when closed.

Bait-casting Reels

These are used in combination with casting rods, but not exclusively (all rods and reels can be interchanged if you so choose). They're used for the boat or pier set up oftentimes. The reel is held atop the rod, as opposed to a spinning reel which sits to one side. When releasing the weighted bait downward, the reel sitting on the top means you can control its up and down movement with ease.

Tripods and Stands

If you are bait fishing as opposed to lure fishing, you'll need something to hold your rods while waiting for a bite. Tripods and stands mostly allow for at least two rods to be placed on them angled toward the wata. In Jamaica I saw anglers take a piece of plastic pipe and push it down into the sand to work on the same principle. Having at tripod or stand frees up your hands to cut more bait or to just sit and chill in between bites and casting.

Once, while fishing on the beach at Dover, I met a guy who was camping out overnight. This is a very common practice among anglers, as night fishing brings in larger and more exotic catches. Plus, camping on the beach is an act of freedom we should all get to experience if safe enough to do so. He dug a hole in the shingle, put his rod in and pushed the shingle back around the rod to hold it steady. Again, same principle, using the local environment as his tools.

Rod Holders

These are used when fishing from a pier generally. The railings along the side of the pier won't have rod holders built into them like on a fishing boat. The holders are a firm piece of plastic (sometimes with an additional material strap), shaped to hold the rod against a railing and stopping it from tipping over the edge when you get a bite. They are easily attached and removed.

Hooks

Consider me strange, but the hook is such a powerful image. What is fishing without a hook? It must be on the end of your line to catch any fish. Its purpose and design speak to the art of fishing and make me consider what I have hooked myself onto over the years – and what needs unhooking. An example of how we've peaked in human design really.

They are a curved piece of metal with a sharp pointed tip and a shorter barb underneath that faces the opposite direction. This additional barb ensures fish are hooked whether they pull backward or forward. Each hook has an eye that your line goes through and is then secured with a knot.

Lake and canal fishing require barbless hooks. This is because fishing here is mostly on a catch-and-release basis. Without the additional barb, you can better ensure the least amount of harm is caused to the fish you plan on releasing once caught.

Now you can have a j-hook, a circle hook, treble hooks, or an Aberdeen hook, with even more sizes of each to match. I generally use a size 1/0 [manufacturers sizes do vary, as well as the shape of hooks – so use measurements which are universal if needed] which are all-rounders. But simply, smaller hooks are for fish with smaller mouths and larger hooks for larger-mouthed fish. Be careful when handling hooks – they're designed *not* to easily be removed.

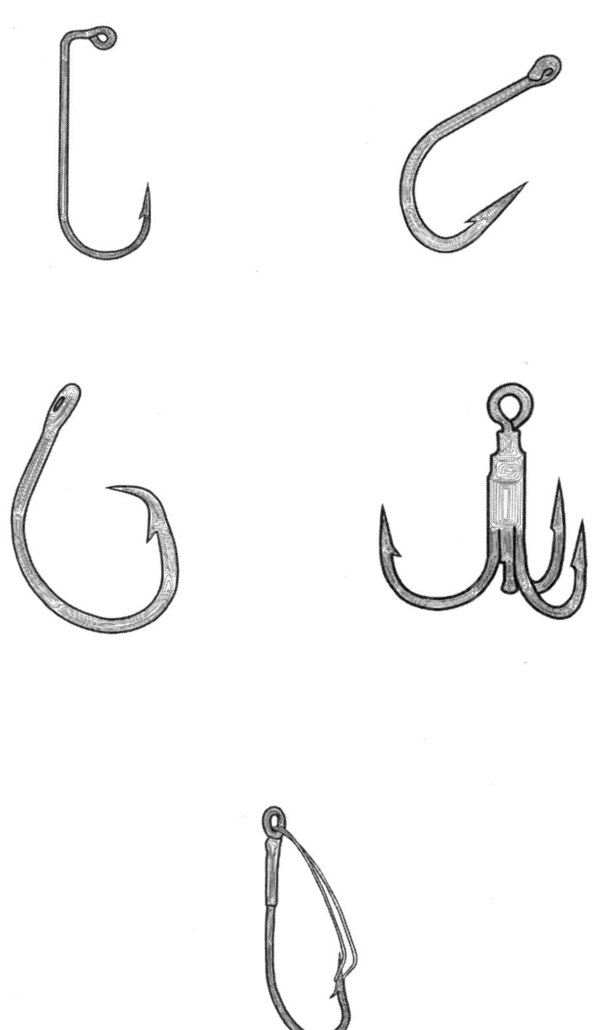

Rigs

A rig is a ready-made set of hooks attached together on one section of line, which can then be easily baited and attached to your main line. I love a two-hook flapper rig – this means there are two hooks attached to this rig that basically flap in the wata column waiting for a bite. There are other rigs like a pulley pennel rig, which is two hooks that work together on one piece of bait. Or there's a bomb rig, which is used on boats to ensure the baited hook or lure doesn't get twisted around the line as it travels through the depths, and naturally spins on its journey.

As one end of your rig is attached to your main line (or leader – but I'll explain this further – *see* page 36), the opposite end will be attached to your weight, making the whole setup complete.

Last week my uncle came round to fish overnight. By that I mean this mixed heritage man from Peckham camped on the beach in December with his tent, rods, cosy sleeping bag and cooking facilities from one morning to the next. Before he set off, we got through a few coffees at my dining room table, and he showed me how to make my own flapper rig. I'm trying to cut down on buying plastic every day now, so this was a welcome lesson. As you get more confident in fishing, give yourself the task of making your own rigs. The art of creating is also a part of the fishing process. You can watch YouTube tutorials and use online resources for step-by-step rig making.

If you're going to buy ready-made rigs, then the hook will be a part of them. There are rigs with one hook attached for, say, live-bait fishing or with two and three hooks for your average day when you're not sure what fish you're likely to catch. When fishing all year round you'll get to know which rig to use for the different species you are targeting.

Rig Wallet

So here I am, 10+ years into fishing, and still – *still* – I pack down from a session and stuff a used rig into my backpack, only to get home and have to cut the hook from the bag's lining. A rig wallet separates your rigs into plastic slips you can close. This stops them tangling with themselves and other rigs, as well as safely securing the hooks and not allowing them to hook onto everything. There are also foam rig holders, where the tip of the hook goes into the foam and the rest of the line wraps around it. Now, for anyone with the kind of ADHD this may speak to – the foams come in different colours so you can colour code your rig setup!

Feathers

Feathers are a rig with anywhere from 4 to 10 small hooks attached. The hooks are dressed in feathers or similar materials like tinsel, designed to imitate small baitfish. When they are moved through the wata column, either by reeling them up or across, they will look like a small shoal moving together as smaller fish do, which predatory fish will naturally chase.

Lines

The two types of fishing line that dominate are monofilament and braided. The former is made from a single strand of nylon, which is easier to handle and less finicky when tying your knots, as it has a more solid structure with a slight stretch to it. The braided line is made from tightly woven synthetic fibres, making it more agile in movement and sensitive to its environment, but can tangle more easily. A lot of rods/reel combos come with the line already spooled tightly on the reel, which is great for beginners and general ease. As you become more used to one type of line, you may want to swap to another. There are lots of videos online to show how best to do this.

I personally like braided lines, as they are super strong but remain sensitive, so spotting a bite in, say, choppier weather is easier. The sea in the UK is mostly choppy to match the weather. Braid can snap when it rubs against rocks or fish with sharp teeth though, so having a leader liner (below) made of mono attached to the end of the braid (which you then attach your rig to) supports the strength of the set up. Leaders also let you switch easily between rigs and lures.

Leaders

Leader lines are shorter sections of line added to your main lines. They are usually more resistant to the abrasions caused by rocks and fish teeth.

Let's take an example. You're lure fishing with the aim of a catching a bass, and casting into an area that is rocky – the best place to find them! But your main line already has an 18-lb (8-kg) braid on it. This is where a leader comes in. You can add a few feet of 20-lb (9-kg) mono line (your leader line) and then attach a snap swivel (Snap swivels have a safety pin-like fastener, or 'snap hook', linked to a crane swivel, which allows quick detachment and interchanging of different lures) to the end so you can easily swap between lures while fishing and test which kind the fish are most attracted to.

Quick Link Leaders

Now these are my personal go-tos when bait fishing from the shore. Quick link leaders already have a crane swivel (this is a terminal tackle component that connects a fishing line to a leader, hook, or lure, designed to prevent line twist by allowing free and smooth rotation under tension.) that you knot onto your main line and a snap swivel on the other end so you can easily change your rigs or lures when fishing. They save some extra knot tying. But importantly – very importantly – knowing how to connect these with knots is crucial to fishing. (We'll go into tying knots in the next chapter.)

Remember, the stronger the fish you're aiming for, the stronger the line you'll need. I use a 30-lb (13.6-kg) braid religiously, as I fish for food as well as sport. Just about everything I try to catch and keep is secured with this strength. Start with under 30lb as your main line and stick with it a while. Buying up everything in the shop at the start of your journey is common but remember the four basics of fishing (*see* page 25). It's simpler than we often make it.

Weights

Your weight has an important triple use. You need the weight to cast out your line, then to get your bait to sink, and finally to anchor the line while waiting for that bite. There are a variety of sizes, but let's break down the kinds of weight, as the sizes will depend on the what the rod can handle.

Gripper Weights

These are used for beach/shore fishing. When you've cast out your line and it hits the sea floor, the gripper weights' arms hook into the sea floor, keeping your setup in place. The current can easily move the weight around, if not. The gripper weight holds your line at one end and you with the rod on the other, creating a tension that you want to keep because it means you can spot when a fish picks up your bait and pulls on the line. You see this as movement in the rod's tip. We'll look at this bite indication in The Fishing chapter.

Sinker Weights

These are weights that don't have the arms that grip into the terrain. You can still use these when coastal fishing, but they are best when you have enough space so that when they move with the current, they aren't interacting or crossing anyone else's line and becoming tangled. The benefit of using a sinker without grippers is that the bait can cover more ground instead of being static, held on the sea floor. If you are boat fishing, you want a sinker weight over a gripper as you hold the rod waiting for the bite. You may be drifting on the boat, so you don't want to be attached to the seafloor while that is happening.

Your rod will have the weight recommendation on the side of it and you want to stick to this, so you don't pressure your rod with too much weight. The recommendation will account for the weight size you should use, to provide the best casting and retrieving performance, and maintain the rod's ability to bend without snapping under too much pressure. When you also factor in line size [lb] it can become a mind field of information. To ease this, start with a Fishing Starter Kit that comes packed with a rod and reel (with the line already spooled on), the weight and lures. This is how you can get straight into fishing, while coming back to these references to expand your set up. No angler, after years of fishing, has just one rod and reel. As your fascination grows so will your need to make space in your yard!

For either kind of weight, the strength of the wind, which you'll be able to gauge by how the line moves – or doesn't – through the air when you cast out, determines the size weight you use at the time. On a calm day, you can go lower. If it's windier and/or you're using bigger bait, you may need to go up. We'll discuss that more in detail when we talk about casting later in the book (*see* page 101).

Lures and Bait

Lures

Lure fishing is to fish without bait. When lure fishing, the weight is generated from the lure instead of an additional weight you attach. Metal lures are heavier, so they sink and flutter up and down in the wata column as you retrieve them. This combination of the fluttered sinking and retrieving mimics an injured fish. Most other lures are designed to move through the column or on top of it. These are made from either firm (on top wata) or soft plastic (for moving through it) and are mostly lighter and therefore better used when the wind conditions are calmer. Lures can be shaped and painted to look like frogs, flies, prawns, worms and anything else that fish eat.

My partner is a big fan of lure fishing and caught a seabass on a soft plastic lure from the shore – something of legends. It can be a very exciting way to fish as the moment a larger fish takes the lure, it gives you direct contact with the bite while the lure is moving. A good selection of lures will help you switch them up during each session to test what fish are after that day. Try bright colours in murkier or deeper wata's and heavier lures in windier conditions.

Bait and Cut Bait

When fishing using bait in the UK, it's common to use lugworm, ragworm, squid and mackerel (but not exclusively). Your local tackle shop will sell these fresh or frozen and stock what's most popular for the fish species in that area. However, the beauty of fishing means you can catch your own bait. For example, when the mackerel arrive on the UK shoreline in the millions (anglers will be lined up on beaches and piers), you can catch up to 20 per person, per day (UK regulations) and store them in the freezer for the rest of the year. In my opinion, they're also one of the best-tasting fish when fresh. These baits, whether they're worms, or the caught mackerel cut into strips, are attached to your hook and cast out into the sea. They release natural oils and scents that draw in fish to take a bite, and you then hook them by using a striking action with your rod. (There is more detail on how to strike later in this book – *see* page 127). Another option for the more experienced – as it needs to be done quickly – is live baiting. This is when you catch a small fish and thread a large circle hook [at least 1/0 and up] through its mouth before dropping it over the side of the boat or casting out from the beach and waiting for a larger predator to come along, swallow the fish and in turn take the hook into its mouth, which you'll strike to hook.

Which bait you use has no hard and fast rules, but there are a lot of die-hard favourites. Meat like fish and bacon can be used to catch crabs. Then there are artificially made flies, made from little pieces of metal with stuck-on feathers that have been delicately designed to look like a fly that has accidently landed on a river or a lake. You can also use insects, shrimp, boilies (special round fishmeal pellets) for carp, fish guts and sweetcorn – the list is endless.

A great rule is to follow the ecosystem. If you're on a beach, then try and use what already lives there. Look for shellfish (the empty shells are an indication of what you can find) and sand crabs, which are both most sustainable and cost-effective choices. What is already there is what the fish will be hunting for, spending a lifetime on the hunt while mapping out areas over hundreds of miles in their lifetime. Just like we know which is the best local food spot for a particular dish, so do the fish know what food is available and where.

Try and experiment with different lures and baits as you go. The different bait you use and how you use it will be a growing source of information on your fishing journey. Try and use some fresh bait if you can – if you catch a small fish, cut off a fillet to use as cut bait, and always have a few lures just in case. Try combining your different baits in one wrapped-up parcel offering scent and structure for your hook.

Bait Elastic

This is a top tip for combining your baits and holding them tightly in one form when casting and sitting in the wata while waiting for that bad-boy bite. You can take a whole squid or a cut piece and fill it with razor clam, mussels or soft-shell crab and then wrap it up burrito-style, using bait elastic. This traps the scent that draws in the fish from the softer meat inside the firmer meat of the squid, so it isn't eaten off by small fish or even dissipated by the current. It's easily digestible for the fish and biodegradable.

Pliers, Knife and Chopping Board

Of the three, I'm most annoyed when I forget my pliers. Some species of fish can have sharp fins and some have rough skin. Using pliers to grab the hook and remove it from the fish is ideal. We'll talk about that later in the book when we get into the heart-pounding magic of catching (*see* page 134)! A knife means you can fillet fish to use as freshly cut bait or bleed fish you want to keep. A chopping board is used the same way as in the kitchen, as it offers a flat surface to work on. But you can always use what's around you if you don't have one – your cooler box lid or look for a large flat rock.

Storage Solutions

Have you ever seen an angler on a mission, with two straps across the shoulders or a large bag strapped across their chest? All armpits full and maybe even a cooler box being pulled behind them? I started my angling career by bringing most of the gear I owned. After time, as you do, I began whittling it down to the basics. You can be most efficient by considering how your gear will be stored for travelling and making sure you bring a good selection of tools that aren't getting mixed up with each other and that you *actually* use most often.

Fishing Bag

The number 1, A1 storage solution you can have. When you arrive at your spot, you may need to scope it out a little. Have a walk to find your temporary resting place for the next few hours. Walk past other anglers to get some space or walk up some steps or a hill for a better view of what shows up in the tide, like any sandbanks or reefs. Having a backpack or bag you can sling over your shoulder(s) frees your hands. They're also designed with a good number of separate sections and pockets to help you organize your gear separately.

Tackle Box

If you're using lures, a tackle box is your best friend. Ten lures with treble hooks all in one case or container will turn into one interconnected clump quickly and seemingly on purpose. Having fewer lures helps, but if you know you want to try out a good few, a tackle box is a great storage solution that keeps each lure separate. It's also useful for storing your lures at home this way as well.

Landing Gear

To help catch fish – especially if lure fishing or on a pier – you may need a net to land them. Your rig or leader lines swivel will reach the first eye of the rod but no further. You may still need to get the fish closer to you, so a net can span the extra space and safely bring your fish in.

Cool Box

Now I usually reserve a cool box or cooler for boat trips. You have a higher chance of catching more fish when the skipper can drive the boat right to where a shoal of fish, a wreck or a reef is, and you drop your line right into the mix. If you're on that boat for eight hours, the fish you've caught needs to be stored in a cooler, preferably with ice. You can also keep your snacks and drinks there too. If you're on a trip and have landed a lot of fish, add some saltwater to the ice to create an ultra-cold, slushy liquid, which can stay that way for days. On the beach, the cooler acts in the same way, but I would go for a smaller one for ease of transportation. It can also triple up as a chopping board or seat.

Safety Gear

Waders, wellies or waterproof boots do what they say on the tin. For example, they keep you dry when fishing on a river if you need to step (safely) into it. I've fished in my trainers more times than not from the beach. When casting out using a long-beach caster rod, there isn't any reason to get into the wata if you don't want to. But I do have a set of waders to use when the tide is low and I want to be knee deep to compensate for the distance of the shallower depth.

Never step into wata if you can't see the depth, and don't walk out too far into the tide just because it seems low. It is powerful and the waves, although usually rhythmic, can break the rhythm sometimes and surprise you with height and power.

If you're fishing alone, take your phone. I've often pulled up and felt the desire to leave my phone in the car, so I'm not tempted to see what the socials are saying instead of being present, but your phone is also a safety tool. You might need it to call the emergency services for someone in trouble, as well as for yourself.

Any boat you're on should legally have a life jacket for each person aboard. You can be an excellent swimmer, but life jackets are not about how well you can swim. If you went in unintentionally (which most people do when not intentionally swimming), not only could you injure yourself, which could affect your ability to swim or tread water, but the current could pull you a great distance very quickly.

Sunglasses are important as they stop the glare of the sun, which can impair your vision. I also find they help to stop me from squinting on overcast days, which gives me tension headaches.

Tide Times

It's important to talk about tide times. This heartbeat-like pulse of the wata is made by the moon and the sun's combined gravitational pull on the Earth. The pull creates a bulge in our planet's wata as it spins on its axis. We experience that as the tide coming in toward us and then away again a few times a day. Whenever you're fishing into a body that is tidal, knowing when it floods (it has risen – high) and ebbs (it has receded – low) will allow you to mark when and how to fish it. Whether it is flooding or ebbing, the two hours either side are when the wata has the largest movement and pressure, activating the fish to feed or move. So, this is a good time to plan your session around.

I use a yearly tide book I got from my local tackle shop. It's a little yellow booklet listing the two high and low tides of the day (some months there are days when there may not be four tides) and the sunrise and sunset times. I use all these bits of information together.

Here's an example. Say I want to fish for mackerel during the summer month of July. On 21 July the evening high tide (when the tide is at its highest point and deepest) will be at 20:44. The two hours before, from 18:44, to the two hours after, 22:44, is when the tide has the greatest amount of movement indicating best chances of catching fish being activated and on the feed with the current. Coupled with the mackerel species being most active at dusk and dawn – this would make between 18.44 and 22.44 on this day when I aim to fish.

Now keep in mind that I am in the UK where tides are likely to happen four times a day (two high and two low). In the Bay of Fundy in Canada there are huge differences in the height of the low and high tides, like here. But the Mediterranean Sea has a tide that hardly changes and it is therefore not such an important factor when you are choosing the optimum time to fish. But the time of day is usually still a factor. Learning about tide times is learning about the moon, the sun and everything's relationship to it. It's a beautiful gift to "sea" what's happening!

Safety Note: Estuaries, sandbars and rocky spots can be dramatically affected by the tide. Always get local information from groups and online searches about the place you intend to fish. What looks like a beach with the tide out at a distance can change quickly and you don't want the tide to cut you off or envelop you. We'll look at this more depth in the Terrain section of this chapter (*see* page 61).

What You Pack Matters

A few years ago, I went to Jamaica for a three-month trip, with the intention of arranging my nationalization and taking the opportunity to fish as much as possible. I planned to fit it in between relishing the unmistakable flavour of freshly grated and squeezed coconut in the rice and peas (way more intense and sweeter than the tin or block version we get in the UK), the three-hour waiting times for bank appointments that should take no more than a few minutes, and adapting to the relentless heat that's right there waiting for you as you make your first turn from the cool haven of your home into the streets. That heat sits directly on your skin as though focused only on you, making Jamaica feel so fiery and alive.

I was going to take this coastal fishing hobby (or should that be obsession?) to the tropical waters of my family heritage. Now, I'd fished in Jamaica before by making friends with the local fisherman in Falmouth on a random stop for a beer years ago. It started as a small payment, a gesture to hitch a ride on a couple of fishing trips, so I could immerse myself in the open-sea wildlife. It morphed into them realizing I was back for yet another day and so becoming a wide-eyed and hopeful but perhaps not-physically-as-able deck hand. But this particular trip was different. This trip I packed for!

One suitcase had my normal stuff: hot girl clothes, everyday clothes, beach clothes and my just-a-quick-stop-for-cornmeal-porridge-in-the-morning clothes. The majority of which I never wore. The other suitcase was entirely full of fishing gear – bar some other tech things like a camera, my speaker and a bag full of tangled chargers. I'm talking about one large suitcase filled and slightly overweight with fishing gear.

Each trip to the beach, by all intents and purposes, should have been about relaxing on the white sand along with the families eating fried fish with bammy and a DJ playing reggae on the largest speakers you'll ever see. But there was I, the "gyal fram farin" as I was lovingly known. Traipsing across these magical vibes on soft sand carrying a backpack and two fishing rods. In the blazing equatorial sun of Jamaica, where time is experienced as more a theory than an absolute. I found myself hot-stepping it along a beach, as though I was getting from one end of the London Tube line to the other in rush hour – head down, uncomfortable and determined. As I dropped this weight I was carrying to the sand, which I had convinced myself must be carried for the third time in as many days, I started to remove the contents I'd feverishly stuffed in piece by piece, a visual demonstration of the unconscious act of holding way too much.

Packing and unpacking has given me the perspective to see how I have lived. Seeing this backpack full of what I do and don't actually need, and not being able to tell the difference for so long, gave me the high-res snapshot needed. You know that scene in a movie where there's more pictures than anyone could hold, now scattered around them while they're kneeling on the floor, right in the centre of it all. They look intensely at the borders of each, and colours that blend and those that need separation, and the faces or places to focus in or out of. Knowing they'll see what's not yet clear within the chaos, until a clue unlocks this current stage and takes them on to the next.

A practise in seeing what my components and parts were, and what's in my bag that never even belonged to me. I get to pack and unpack like a religion now. A church if you will.

After that day in Jamaica, I started to travel lighter. When it comes to essential packing for what goes in my bag, I've found a sweet spot.

These are my go tos, as they're needed the most and, with them, I can make all kinds of fishing happen even if unexpected changes to plans come up:

- Grip Weights – remember to make sure the weight is suitable for the rod.
- Rigs – a couple of two-hook flapper rigs, a set or two of feathers, a flattie rig and probably a pulley pennel rig in case I need larger cut baits or a live bait.
- Tide times guide or online info – I like those four hours either side of the tide when the wata/tide is moving the most.
- Quick link leader – a few for quickly switching between rigs or lures.
- Dish cloth or small towel – to clean my hands and for holding fish that may have sharp fins.
- Fishing pliers – for removing the hook from fish and usually doubling as scissors.
- Knife – for chopping up bait and dispatching fish and bleeding them.
- Lures – just 2 lures can be enough (to give it a couple casts) if you're not planning on lure fishing and you don't have a lure rod with you.

Now let me share with you some items I've brought over the years that I'm yet to use, do not know what they are used for or have used once and never again:

- Box of 500 hooks – I have hooks in every imaginable size, of which at least 100 are so small my ageing eyes couldn't thread a line through the eye without those one-size-fits-all glasses you try on while waiting for your prescription in the pharmacy.
- Head-lamp-style skull cap – bought from a petrol service station somewhere because I thought it would make a great addition to the gear when night fishing. After 10+ years of fishing and even living a stone's throw from a beach, I have never fished overnight.
- Squid lights – Bought a three-pack of lights to drop into the sea in the evenings when squid fishing, to attract said squid and increase

my chances of catching them. None of these have ever tasted salt water, even if I could work out how to get them to alight. Yet I have managed to catch squid even without trying to catch them!

However, there are fishing items and paraphernalia that as I've become a more experienced angler have come to life in their meaning. For example, those glow-in-the-dark end stoppers. I had a box of a hundred of them as part of a fishing gift set my partner gave to me years ago. I would open it occasionally and take one out into the palm of my hand, which I closed tightly around it, and then peek through a tiny slit made with my thumb and finger. One eye closed and one peeking through the slit, I would check it still glowed each time. I knew it would come in handy for something, but I had no idea what it was supposed to be used for. Then, not long ago, Uncle Glen invited me on a boat trip to fish the wrecks and banks deep in the English Channel. This trip was exclusively for his fishing "crew" – men, older, experienced and with the kind of jokes where the punchline means *his* is smaller or larger than *his*. I was entertained with British humour, the most elite of its kind in my humble opinion, but also hoping no one brought up their political views.

While I was chaka chaka-ring with my rod and rig set up, not at all used to fishing in 90feet (27m) of wata with my own gear, I excitedly set up on the kitchen table the night before with some wine and 90's R&B sounds. One of the guys said "Here, come here luv. Let me help you out there", with pity and kindness and a little misogyny wrapped in one. He immediately cut my main line with his small scissors connected to a pulley string on his belt, allowing it to drop to the floor of the boat without looking down to acknowledge it. And, with some weaving of magic with his hands made a boom rig that allowed one long line with a large hook on the end to go down to the depths with the weight attached. At the top of this rig, close to the first eye of the rod, there was a glow-in-the-dark end stopper. That day I found out that they're in fact used to stop the crane swivels and swivel hooks from hitting that first eye and damaging it. They glow in the dark because at depths like this, they will attract curious fish as well.

It's like that. You can have and hold something for years and peek at it every so often until it's ready to reveal its true purpose. Or until your purpose matches with it.

When you fall in love with this thing we call fishing, you will want to take it all in; the videos, the chats, the experiences, the gear, the clothing, maybe even the head lamp-style skull cap, and I recommend you do. We must be bags full of our past and future selves, as we do our work at the wata's edge, figuring out how to be a container for the present.

Every Song Has a Hook

I don't see how I can write this book about the art of fishing, without sharing a weight I have carried my entire life that brought me to the wata, as part of my internal work. It's the kind of hook that sticks deep into the skin and makes pulling away even worse – a weight that as a child was so unbearable, my spirit learned to leave its body and be suspended in a place where you wait until it's safe enough to return. But each time it returned to its container, it felt less of a fitting space, as though either the spirit or the body was changing form without true partnership and symbiosis with the other. I remember as a child trying to explain with limited vocabulary to my easily spooked grandmother that I was too big for the room, or sometimes the opposite – that I was too small for the room and she must try and understand me as best she could, as this was an urgent matter of being in an incorrect shape inside these walls that are closing.

I have a lead investigator now, who took over from the previous lead investigator, before my very first lead investigator was assigned to my case. The last email I received informed me there was a corruption in the software, which meant the case had to be re-uploaded to the new system before being handed to the CPS (the UK Crown Prosecution

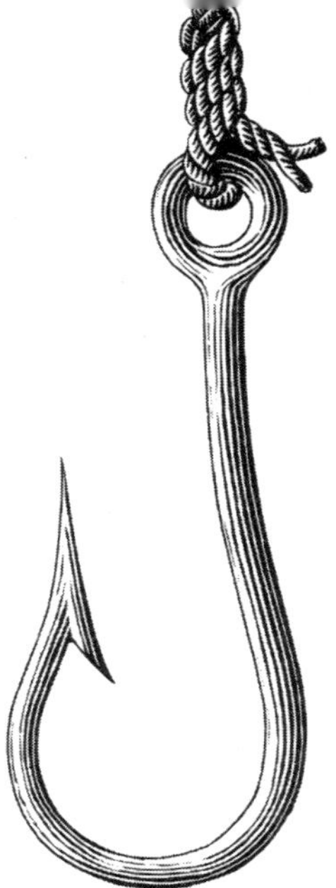

Service) who would decide on A, B or C – a game show of possibilities to what will happen for me next. Before it was originally uploaded (and now again) it included the transcript of my statement, given to two wonderful CAIT officers (**Child Abuse Investigation Team** within a UK police force) who visited me at home, just a little outside of London, in 2020. They wore plain clothes – I remember that. I offered them tea and they accepted. I was nervous and focused on the task of tea-making as a calming mechanism. You know when you make it special. Two cups with a tea bag in each, a little bowl of sugar with two teaspoons, the tiny pitcher used only for times like this to hold just enough milk for each, and a dish for the discarded tea bags when they reach optimum seeping consistency.

They explained that they didn't want to sit in front of me and take notes, so instead would use an inconspicuous camera to capture us in more of a conversational style. They said apologetically from the beginning that they would need as much detail as possible. We sat for an amount of time I have no true reflection of, as I gave my statement, with as much detail as possible.

This file with my personal statement also includes statements from those in my life at the time I was being abused, as well as those who have known me since, who have listened actively at 3am when the rum told me to be brave and share the shame with friends who have stopped me from falling, or breaking in half completely. Who can confirm "yes, she falls somewhere below ground sometimes, into herself and stays coiled because of this, what was done to her" while they whisper "stay here" in my ear, or in text messages when they need to. An example of how love holds us. It includes school reports to help give context, on what a child who feels they can longer fit their spirit into their body, presents as. In historical cases like mine, there is no tangible evidence akin to a true crime documentary when the officers walk in to see the coffee table is flipped, after noting the front door being left ajar. In these historical cases, context is all we have. Who we could have been if they have never been. When we changed. When we spilt. Separated.

This file has lived on the desk of those officers for years now. I know it sits among many files with many names written in the space at the front made for names to fit neatly into. Those files, I suspect, have stayed on their desks alongside the coffee cup that says "Best Dad" and pen holders with highlighters that help investigators connect the dots.

Before my file lived on their desk and in their system, that file lived within me. I was the keeper of those stories, just like the wata.

At the age of around 30, I was watching an interview with a man who used to be a dancer for a well-known popstar in the 80's. He was being interviewed by a woman I do not remember. As I focused in on the conversation, the interviewer asked, "Why say something now – it's been so many years?" or something to that effect. He responded that if anyone had asked him back then, he would and did say "Nothing happened", an answer some of us will understand. He then went on to explain that for some reason, when becoming a married man with children of his own, that one day – like awakening from a long coma – he remembered. Those words, in that moment, broke the alien shape I had been trying to hold my entire adult life. Like him, I was awakened, and I spilled out of the seams. I spilled out onto the bed in that one-bedroom flat in Brixton and it left my muscles and cartilage trembling. Every inch of my body vibrated as I realized the only place I had known as home – my body – was separate from my spirit all this time. Looking at myself scattered on the soft carpeted floor like a 10,000-piece puzzle, lamenting at how I would ever get myself back together. The memories I had were in front of my mind's eye as clearly as an expensive home cinema set up. I had to rewatch these movies again. Something I would later have to retell and retell and retell to allow them to be part of my story, not the only story as I let them be free from shame.

That day, rewatching the memories trapped inside the cells of my body of my first perpetrator, putting his index finger across his top and bottom lip, communicating to me without speaking, to not say anything. He and I made an agreement that I was too innocent to have legally signed. On one of these nights, where time pauses and the digital clock tells the same time for far too long, so I instead scan for hidden messages in the patterned wallpaper. I do that magic trick, where the psyche peels itself away from its walls, like the decorator once did on the walls my eyes are now fixed upon. In this place, the imagination is as vast as the Pacific Ocean. Uncharted. I somehow hear my grandmother's voice calling me as though its real. In that way she did, when she wanted to know why I had done what I said I had not. I've now left my body behind like groceries at the till as I make a dash for that one last thing, and am standing at the bottom of the stairs in her house looking up at her. She is standing at the top, with one hand on her hip, where it rested as an anchor to hold down all the feelings she had learned to contain. "Come up stairs now," she said in her old age Jamaican accent, her eyes squinting and focused. In this place, the uncharted place, I was perhaps travelling through time and space to meet those who have travelled there before me. She was telling me to move. Forward, upward, anyhow. But I was not ready yet in those years to do so. So, like the lineage I arrived from, I continued a cycle of holding the secrets others leave on us, weighing us down with the baggage we would one day have to look at and learn to separate piece by piece.

"The universe makes no mistakes" say the spiritually inclined. A huge and far-reaching concept to sit with and believe in, but one that does bring me comfort. It's OK to want comfort. It's OK to give it to ourselves, I'm learning. But this concept doesn't always do the job of comfort I have requested and needed from it. My anger and need for justice come in direct opposition to this theory sometimes, but on a soul level it feels like wata and not burning fire, at least.

Separating from your own seams for so long did eventually become tiring to me, and those I was attempting deep relationships with. It took a lot of time, of holding, and hearing, and healing, to feel like my own shape fits me and I fit into the shape of rooms again, and for the fire to not burn anyone who dared to touch.

I'm guessing this is why I fell in love with the art of fishing. Fishing was an act of saving myself without feeling so alone, because the wata feels like everyone, all at once. An equalizing. Being given a focus point for the minutiae of fishing, the small pieces that fit together to make one rig, and how the rig connects the line that runs through the eyes of the rod. How I sat – and still do – for hours at a time, with just my thoughts, not caring about the bite indication, but the need for peace or the childlike excitement each time I do catch a fish. Because what I caught, was on my own terms. What I hooked, I sometimes returned. Giving myself the choice of what stories I release back to the wata and what stories I take with me. Now I move forward, upward, anyhow, while I decide how my fishing session will go. I don't need to run away. I can sit with it, which to the stories of my ancestors farther reaching then my own grandmother's is a revolutionary act. I mean, after me, there will be no more daughters anyway.

The last session I had with my therapist before I took a break to start EMDR (Eye Movement Desensitization and Reprocessing), a form of therapy to help process trauma {a break, ha!}, he stood at the doorway after we hugged goodbye, and I turned back for the last "See you soon", in that multilayer of vocal stimming of goodbyes we do. He said "Hey, next time we do a session, let's do it while fishing".

THE SET UP

"Nuh wait till drum beat before yuh grine yuh axe."

With fishing, the ritual begins before your hook and line make contact with the wata. You'll need to know where your grand production will take place and what tools you'll need to create this movie *you* get to direct. Consider the beach you visit as your set; the weather on the day is your lighting; and the moments you take to reflect on are why this movie – *your* movie – deserves to be made. The research you do before arriving becomes the script, each take, your practice, and any with additional edits you get to make each time. What an honour that we get to discover how this great expanse of our planet moves, what moves in it and how it can move us!

Finding the right fishing spots allows us to unlock this newfound passion or, as many people have shared with me over the years, a revisiting of the time spent with their fathers. Perhaps they were too young to see the togetherness this brought about at the time, but they are being called back to it again. It might be a dormant ancestral skill that your family was known to use, at a time before you existed, in a place different to the one you call home now. It's about the research, the listening, using your intuition, and the childlike sense of adventure we get that reinvigorates us.

We've heard the shouts of concern and seen the real time effects of this digital age of Aquarius. Our distractions keep us avoidant, head-down, socially watchful, yet not quite social. The phones and A.I will apparently take our jobs and our lives if we let them. But as we head into unprecedented times, where having skills that sustain us becomes even more important, the art of fishing can offer us re-connection to the green and blue spaces *while* using this access to information we hold in our hands as a tool. We don't need to avoid our own evolution as a species to also remember who we are. I was speaking with my partner last night about our journeys of healing. There was a point we both remembered with laughter to soothe the mortification in the memory of when we started talking therapies like CBT, (cognitive behavioural therapy – a form of psychotherapy that helps individuals change unhelpful thinking and behaviour patterns to manage mental health conditions and emotional concerns) and were allowed to hear our own fears and goals and secrets never yet spoken aloud for the first time. With that, our first step in the journey was learning to be kinder to ourselves. Not speaking for so long creates a lot of shame. Our shame wants to hide behind our ego - the powerful and fierce versions of ourselves we create to keep that shame safe. When we become kinder to ourselves, what can arise is are phrases like *'you're just projecting your issues onto me'* in response to someone who's sharing something we may not be ready to hear about our own behaviour. Projecting being the word we just learnt, to help understand the thing we don't yet understand. Joining the kind of spiritual mafia crew, where it must be someone else fault, because we must be kind to ourselves first for the healing to take place. The muscles we're developing to release the shame, springs into action at every chance it gets. But eventually after more of the work and more revealing of the layers, we can then start to separate what is shame that should be released and/or returned, and what is some shame we have to sit with in that therapy session, {as our therapist reminds us to collect our chins from the floor}. We move into, *I have hurt others as well as being hurt myself.*

Like a form of therapy, learning to fish doesn't come all at once, and it doesn't come because we completely change our day-to-day life instantaneously. We don't need to throw the baby out with the bath water to become better anglers and closer to our natural source. We use what we have and start where we are.

My favourite unofficial coaches are ones who share their fishing videos on YouTube. There's a huge community of anglers, foragers and catch-and-cookers, whose visual style helps me to imagine myself in the performance before it's started for me. Seeing how different people have learned to cast to suit their bodies is a reminder to let the motion work for you, not against you. There's that moment in a World Cup final when it all comes down to penalties and the fated player walks up to the ball, looks at it, looks at the goal, then back at the ball, before launching the hopes of their nation into the back of the net. Scientists have described this as *mental imagery*. The spiritually inclined call it "seeing with your mind's eye". For me it's the gym on my couch that adds to the understanding of the movements I'll make, and it's what my partner already knows I'll be watching before entering the living room.

Like YouTube, Facebook groups where anglers inform you what's good fishing in a particular area in real time are gold, as fish species move in migration as temperatures rise and fall. It's great to know when the squid have arrived on your shores, as that's free bait that can be frozen for the rest of the year, as well as a tasty meal that can be cooked up. Tackle shops, where you can get your fresh baits and fishing gear, can be another place to ask questions and gather data when friendly and welcoming, which most are.

But as a Black, queer woman, I haven't always been made to feel comfortable in those spaces or online. In little towns that don't like big changes. Or online where small thinkers need a big audience. This is exactly why my partner and I set up the We Are Black Fish fishing group – a community of us, searching for the same destination – a little piece of peace in the noise that gives us safety in numbers to bring our vibe and culture to the coastline. I hope this handbook acts in the same way, accompanying you as you learn, practise, and fall in love with the art of fishing.

Here are some tips, tools, and knowledge for finding the right spots and feeling like you belong. What to look out for when deciding where to set up and the things to consider before you cast out your line each time.

Which Beach?

Around the coast you'll spot anglers, facing the sea, seemingly in deep meditation and focus. The more you become a part of this angling community, the more you'll notice them and make note of which beaches look most promising. Choosing which beach to visit, within your range, is about learning the language of the sea and the beach that sits alongside it. We get the chance in this process of discovery to move inquisitively like our ancestors, taking note of what is happening with the elements of earth, air, and water, inspiring us to look up and around.

Our tech-filled, people-filled, media-filled lives are busy and can feel packed into bright orange "bags for life" a lot of the time. You may be fitting this hobby around your work life and the time you have spare to maybe teach and spend quality time with your children, nieces, and nephews. Or grow closer to your partner and friends, and be a part of a community like We Are Black Fish. Start where you are – that's curious and courageous.

Here are some things to look out for when considering which beach you go to for a fishing session.

Wata Quality

I use an app called Surfers Against Sewage, (there is also the US version EPA's How's My Waterway website if you live in America) the evening before or morning of my session to check if there's been any sewage spills. You don't generally see these spills, which go out into the sea via underwater pumps. The "water" utility companies keep their pipe locations as secret as an illuminati Christmas party for good reason. I'm sure if we knew where these pipes were located, we'd likely do what we could to stop them in action. If there is a warning for the beach you've chosen to fish at, it's not ideal but it doesn't *have* to stop you. If you can, support the organisations that are fighting for better regulations on the dumping of waste into bodies of wata.

When coastal fishing, the fish could have been travelling from a distance, moving into the shoreline and back out with the tide as they hunt. Where I am based on the southeast coast of the UK, we share the English Channel with France. The fish here are doing long drives! Because of this, even with a local spillage, it is safe to keep fish for food. Shellfish like mussels, clams and oysters live their lives attached to one structure, so stay away from foraging for them where spills are known to take place. You can still use these shellfish for fresh bait though.

Remember that your eyes and nose are high tech tools. How does the wata and surrounding beach look and smell to you? If you see a lot of trash on a beach and there is an unpleasant funk in the air, then it's likely not the safest or cleanest. It hurts to see this. You may want to pack a spare garbage bag on your fishing sessions to pick up refuse left by others and certainly to collect up your own. As your relationship with the wata becomes deeper, you're reminded of your stewardship in preserving the beach's health.

It's also important to feel safe as this powerful resource can be dangerous. Later (*see* pages 61, 71, 73), we'll talk about weather and beach terrain for additional information on respecting its force.

Google Earth

I saw a video of someone using Google Earth to view the beach for a low tide fish. It showed there was a reef close enough to fish onto when the tide was out. This is something you wouldn't necessarily be able to know before making a day of it. Getting a bird's eye view of a beach this way is now firmly in my tool kit. You can often find me on a train or in between meetings having a Google Earth moment even without immediate plans to visit anywhere. I'm constantly saving and storing info about different beaches. If it's low tide, I may decide to fish on a beach I've seen that has rock exposed, so I can walk out onto the rocks (safely) and lure for some bass or cod, as these fish are strong enough to fight the currents created by the rocks and hunt smaller fish that don't have the same power. Keep in mind, though, that these images are snapshots in time, and terrain changes over the years, so use them as a tool alongside noting the terrain of the beach and the weather that day, which we'll look at further in this chapter.

Social Media

This is a great tool for insider tips on beach access points that are less obvious, like free parking or which side of a pier is better for avoiding underwater rocks and structures you can easily get your gear snagged on. Searching hashtags for the beach you're thinking of visiting that day provides great additional data. That person filming who does the millennial pause at the start of the clip – yeah, they'll likely have some good intel! It's also a way to connect with an angling community.

Vibe Check

Some beaches are quiet and less known while others are the staple go-tos. Walking or driving along the beach before unpacking your gear, if possible, will give you a chance to get the lay of the land. Piers are more likely to bring a little angler conversation, as your gear will be set up closer together to save space. When coastal fishing you'll want to give other anglers a wider berth if you have the choice, so your lines don't get entwined when casting out or reeling in, which makes it likely more of a solitary experience. But remember this is your session. Acknowledge the energy and vibe you're after that day. What do you need from your visit right now? This will change from session to session, so remember to tap into yourself. If you're with friends or family and not everyone has caught the fishing bug like you, think about what the vibe will be for them. Can they swim there? Can you light a BBQ or make a fire pit? Should you pack toys for sandcastle building? What snacks and music do you all want for the belly and the vibes?

Trial and ~~Error~~ Learning

Some beaches just don't feel right, and some may become your second home. I can think of a couple spots I've tried that required too much of a traverse on my ageing knees along a shingle beach. Other spots have become my go-tos for their stunning sunrise or sunsets, facilities that are close enough to access, or I've made some angling friends there who are regulars for likely the same reasons.

Listen, some days, you set up and forget a bit of equipment, which makes things just that bit more difficult. Sometimes you may even blank (catch no fish). But absolutely every time, I've learned something new: where the snags are, what kind of fish species may or may not be in abundance there and some imperative info from an angler on a pier. Keep notes on where you visit.

Which Terrain Am I On?

The terrain of a beach has been shaped over many lifetimes. That slowness has created its painting-like scenery, which can really anchor us and create a stillness the mind and spirit call for. It offers an earthly and solid grounding in a life when we must question how January seemingly jumps to April without even a courtesy email. Those different terrains under the surface have become the cities and towns different fish species have chosen and, like us, have learned to survive and thrive in.

Fishing for different species is something you'll want to do naturally as you seek out new fishing adventures, so looking up, out and around is key to storing this data, and teaches you to take in how wata shapes the land, making the connection between what the beach and the seafloor look like and how they likely mirror each other.

Terrain can change, though. A sandy beach can become a shingle beach after a big storm and then returns to sand just a few days later as the weather settles and resides. High tide can cover rocks and tide pools and bring the action closer to your set up for a restful seated bait fishing session. Low tide can call you to get on those rocks and lure fish right in the action of the swells.

Here are some tips about the different types of terrain you can expect and the fishing you may want to do on them.

Shingle

Shingle beaches are made of stones, small rocks and pebbles created over centuries by the ocean and seas movement. They are more common along the coasts of England, Japan, New Zealand, North America and South Africa. Personally, I love the sound a shingle beach makes when I move across it. One of my favourite sounds is when a car tyre turns on gravel – auditory pleasure. Most beach goers who want a day out are looking for sandy beaches, so shingle beaches are usually the least occupied, particularly come the height of summer or during holidays.

Shingle has steep drop-offs, which is something to keep in mind when swimming, but it means that at high tide, you don't need to cast far out to catch, as fish move across the dips bringing them closer to us. This is good when you're still learning the art of casting, as casting out a fair distance takes practice and confidence.

For a long time while fishing on a shingle beach, I'd always struggle to get my rod holder's legs deep enough into the pebbles to hold them firmly. This meant that after a few casts or lifting and returning the rod numerous times, it started to have that Mary J Blige "I'm-going-down" sway. Or if windy enough, it could collapse and then there was one me, two rods and a rod holder, like the calamity scene in a cartoon! Someone showed me a great trick for securing it though, using either my fishing bag or a spare bag filled with rocks hung on the central hook (most stands have this), which gave it central weight stability. I do this every time now.

In terms of fish species, these will change depending on where in the world you are. In the UK during the summer huge shoals of mackerel arrive at the coastline, while there are cod and bass in the colder months. The terrain, cross-referenced with the migrations of the species, will start to give you an idea of what to fish for each session.

Sand

These beaches are the sun chasers' dream, soft on the feet, welcoming and tropical. In the UK, for a couple months a year we flock to them to take advantage of the northern hemisphere's daylight-saving hours. These sandy beaches are busiest, especially in summer months, unless you are lucky enough to live elsewhere where sandy beaches are in abundance such as around the Caribbean or in the Balearic Sea (between mainland Spain and the Balearic Islands).

Sandy beaches are flatter than shingle, and you can walk out into the sea a fair way. Because of this, it's important to do some research on the movement of the tide as it comes back in for the day. For example, take Camber Sands in East Sussex where, as the tide comes back in, it arrives first behind you (that is, further away from the shoreline and closer to land), which can trap you in the middle and has been known to cause drownings. So, head to sandy beaches as the tide is ebbing (going out), which will give you a good number of hours before it turns and starts coming back in, and do as much research as you can on what it looks like as the tide comes back in before you get there.

You might need to cast out further on a sandy beach if there aren't any drop-offs in the seafloor. So, make sure you have a rod that supports a longer cast, or try switching your reel to a casting multiplier. Put on some waders to allow you to walk a little into the swell to help get your line out further, or wear shorts and water shoes that are made to get wet and stay comfortable on your body.

These sandy beaches have what's called "breaks". Wherever there is a dip or a ledge in the seafloor, the waves hit it and create swells. Where you see the wata is calm, it's deeper. If you are bait fishing, you want to cast into those calmer looking spots, as that's where the fish are moving through as a kind of alleyway. Casting into the swells will whip up your bait, destroying it before fish get a chance to bite.

On sandy beaches, you've got a good chance of catching flatfish like flounder and plaice, as they bury themselves in the sand and wait for a passing feast. But you can also catch crabs that are walking along the seafloor.

Mixed Ground

This is a mix of sand and shingle. You'll mostly see shingle as you approach, but when the tide is out it will reveal the sand. The constant movement and the power of the sea over time will have pushed the rocks up to the shore, creating the dips. The beaches that have larger dips (think little hills of stone), require you to move your gear a couple times closer or further as the tide ebbs and floods. So, keep your gear tidy and together to make those moves easier.

Like the name suggests you'll get a mix of fish species here. Mixed ground often has seaweed and weeds in it, which larger fish hide out or rest in, – one of the reasons it's loved by our spear fisherfolk. You could lure fish across the top, which will give you a good chance of catching a larger predator fish, or cast out a live bait, but be ready to see that rod tip bend. Predator fish are known to take the bait and keep moving, instead of investigating first.

Both sand and mixed ground beaches have various species of clams and worms, which you can forage for. This fresh bait is amazing – any rig you send out with the hook tipped with them will be popular.

Tide Pools and Reefs

These beaches stand out as the rocks and tide pools are visible. Anglers stand on the rocks (waders or boots with a good grip are a must for safety) and lure fish into the choppy wata. Predator fish are most active in these terrains as they can manoeuvre through the swells created by the rocks. For protection in numbers, those small fish tend to move in small shoals (the kind you see when snorkelling on holiday), which makes hunting for larger fish most fruitful in an act of double-dutching into nature's symbiosis, as you jump into the mix, or rather aim for it with your lure.

It's exhilarating luring for and catching a monster fish while the wata crashes against the rocks. Anglers head to places like New Zealand for this reason. This is a seriously visceral and in-the-moment way to fish compared to the calmer and more meditative bait fishing from the shore. It provokes the healthy kind of anxiety our body appreciates. But as visceral as this is, it comes with its dangers, like slipping on the rocks into the wata, or injuring ourselves on sharp edges. When possible, go with someone else. Once you're there and have found your footing, stay solid and planted as much as you can. Again, keep your head on a swivel – if you're going to be so close to the edge, you've got to respect its power by watching constantly, and never turn your back to the wata. Pack extra lures (soft plastics, spoons) and swivels (like snap swivels) to quickly change lures if you get snagged. The rocks are unforgiving and once your hook is snagged, it can be diffcult to retrieve

On a very low tide, like a spring tide, these beaches will reveal a world of crabs, scallops, lobsters, starfish, sea anemones and fossils for a magical and educational foraging session, where you get to see the life usually hidden between the rocks under the surface.

Let's now take a brief look at fishing in different bodies of wata.

Rivers

It's best to avoid entering fast-moving wata, as it's difficult to tell the power just by looking at it. Equally, don't step into anything you don't know the depth of. Look for a calm part of the river to aim your lure into, along the edge where there may be more weeds and branches fish use to congregate and hide in or fallen trees that become breeding grounds. You'll be lure fishing here, so remember to pack light and have minimal gear in your backpack to free up your hands.

Lakes, Canals and Ponds

A lake is a large body of wata being fed by rivers and streams, or rain. They are generally still without waves but can be deceivingly deep. To fish in a lake in both the UK and US you need a license which can be bought from the local council for anything from a day's fishing to a yearly membership. Fishing here can be a calm and healing session with a mixed species population.

Canals can also be walkways for pedestrians, especially in urban areas, so be considerate to them and make sure you don't leave bags and equipment lying around causing obstacles. Otherwise, people with physical difficulties may struggle to see what's on the ground or have to move around you. Canals are fixed body of wata that doesn't always flow out to a larger sea, so wata can be stagnant here, especially in and around cities. If you are fishing in a canal, you are only catching and then releasing fish as they usually contains harmful bacteria if digested.

Fishing ponds are often maintained by a private owner or company. These usually offer fishing sessions you have to pay for. The ponds are stocked solely for the purpose of fishing, so you may need to purchase a day ticket. Research them before you go in case there are stipulations on fishing times and to find out in advance how much they cost.

The Deep Sea

These are inevitably going to be chartered fishing experiences. In just about every country I visit, I book a charter to do some inshore fishing. I choose inshore because the further out into the ocean you go (offshore), the larger the waves can be and the more chance of me becoming seasick. Research a reputable company and consider the time of day you'll be out there, especially when in a hot country. The morning or late afternoon might be a better time than the middle of the day, with less intense sun exposure.

What Is the Weather Like?

UK weather is as chaotic as a three-man podcast. It's also – for us here – very much *ours*, and to be embraced for its changing seasons and the fishing those changes provide. Like countries with a stable yearly climate, you can and should fish all year round in places like the UK, with its four seasons. I know it gets cold in the winter months, but the beauty of being on the beach in winter is the low sun on the horizon without interruption from tall buildings blocking out our well-needed dose of vitamin D. Additionally, the autumn and winter months make for the most fruitful fishing here in the UK.

Rain can dampen the mood if it gets in the way of you looking up, around and at your rod tip, but when was the last time you were in a little rain and emancipated yourself from how it would affect your hair or clothes? Once you get a bite and that excitement sends cortisol rushing through your nervous system, you'll quickly forget about whatever weather you're in. It will feel better than any party or after party and won't leave you hanging on for dear life for the next few days.

Let's look at fishing seasonally and what to keep in mind.

Winter

Yes, it will be cold. I'm prone to cold feet and hands, so thick boots are a must for me. Gloves I'm not so keen on as a neurodivergent person, but if you can wear them, go for ones that allow a good amount of movement or have the little fingertip hoodies so you can easily switch between say, baiting up a hook or changing a rig, and then back into snug town.

Each day the sun hangs low along the horizon making it a golden hour all day. Pack some sunnies during these sessions as the rod tip can be blocked by the sunlight and bait fishing requires a lot of looking at this. In winter it's important to be kind to your body. If it's too cold, don't force yourself to go or stay too long. It defeats the object to not enjoy your session.

Fishing in winter can be just as healing and fruitful as at any other time of year. The beaches are less packed – there are usually just dog walkers (be careful with any bait left dangling, as no one wants to do emergency hook removal on a dog) and a few others stealing a moment by the wata.

The fish species for the coast you have chosen can be researched and kept up to date by checking with online groups for real time data. Having an idea of what you aim to catch will inform you of packing essentials for that session. But also have some across-the-board rigs to experiment with and see what's out there. As our climate is changing, so is the sea temperature. What we've come to know as migration times are now unreliable, as each year throws up surprises about what species are at shorelines earlier or later than expected, if at all, and when they have never been recorded there in previous years.

Summer

There'll be a lot of people on the beach, so think of them. Give them some space and be prepared for people to walk under your line as it sits waiting for action. It's not something to worry about though, as the rod sitting up on the rod stand will be holding the line up higher than an average human being. But be mindful if anyone is passing you when you cast out your rod.

If time permits, you'll probably want to stay out longer in summer, so bring a choice of snacks and beverages. The vibe check (*see* page 60) you were looking for must be adhered to.

Having some feather rigs in your bag, even if you're not focusing on mackerel, herring or sardines that day, is a good idea, as huge shoals of these fish travel along most coastlines at this time of the year. Although you can catch them with even a two-hook flapper rig, feather rigs have five or more hooks to reel in more fish each time before they move on. You can collect them as bait to be frozen or salted for sessions to come, as well as eating them as a sustainable food source.

Rain

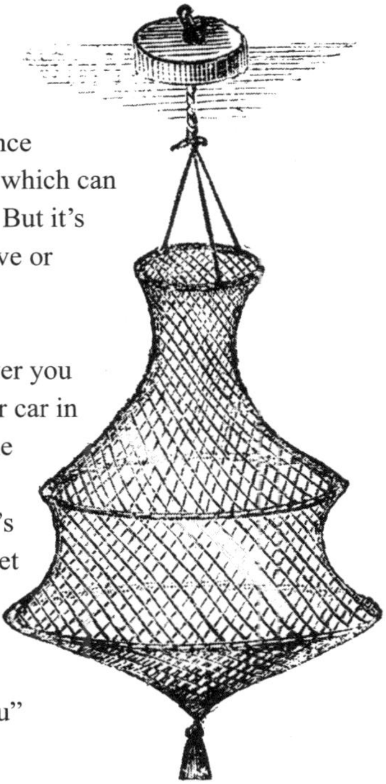

This is more about our fishing experience than the effect on the fish. They do experience some changes in behaviour in heavier rain, which can cool the wata and activate their movement. But it's inconclusive as to whether rain has a positive or negative effect on fishing.

If you are called to let a downpour wash over you (and your soul), like someone washing their car in the rain – always, always do you. That is the free will we ask for, that's available to us, freely. But don't fish during a storm. There's no way of predicting how big a swell can get and you don't want to be taken home, home. Right after a storm is optimal, as crustaceans and worms have been swept up from the seabed creating a "tasting menu" for the fish.

Wind

Now wind is a frenemy to the angler if ever there was one. It churns up the seabed, sous chef-style and creates feeding frenzies, but it can also have your rod tips bouncing so much it's difficult to tell if you have a bite or the thing is just having the time of its life like a dog hanging out of a car window. You should give fishing a try on a windier day though, as it really tests casting skills and helps measure bite indication, which can make it even easier to recognise on those calmer days.

It's worth noting the different wind speeds to understand what works for you and get a sense of what gear you'll need to pack. It's important to see how the weather affects your experience and provides context to the research you've done and information in sources like this book, so it can be truly cemented in your angler tool kit.

Always check the weather conditions before setting off and take note of the wind speed. It can change throughout the day, so you'll need to judge the time it takes to get to your desired location and how long your session will be.

Here are some general guidelines to help you understand how wind speed may affect your fishing:

- Under 10mph you're good. The wata can be like silk, and you can really hear the gentle lapping of waves and birds flying above. Great for a social trip with family and friends and for catching slower moving fish, like flatfish species.
- Up to 20mph and you'll likely have to go up a little in weight and gripper weights to hold your line in one spot. Without a gripper weight your line will move in the current and could get caught up with rocks, objects, your other fishing line if using more than one rod or other anglers either side if you. The swells can offer you ASMR heaven as they meet up against the shore on windier days. But I wear a hoodie, so my neck is protected from the wind.
- 20+mph (48+kph), unless you're on a survival weekend or it is vital for your actual survival, give this a miss. The lines will be

bouncing in the waves, making the rod tip move constantly, and the wind will feel rough on your skin and body at the very least. It may even cause large waves that come in further than expected, making it dangerous. See it, give it a nod of respect and stay home would be my advice.

You can use the weather to learn more about your internal dialogue. It can show you how perfectly designed you are to handle challenges. Rain can be about the need for an internal release and practising your resilience. Wind speed can be about you leaning into your logic by being adaptable – for example, "I need to cast more to the left this time because the wind is carrying it to the right". And the cold is about endurance and commitment. This is a beautiful hobby that teaches us so much about ourselves and allows us to learn in optimal, challenging or less comfortable weather.

Navigating Public Space as a Non-conforming Body

As we know well, it's not the beach that has unspoken restrictions for non-conforming bodies, but the society that has bordered and shaped it. This can mean residents in the small towns in these coastal areas have been less used to diversity and the changing face of people movement than city folks. Some of these individuals can sometimes act like self-appointed police, acting without warrants or need. So, we must consider how we safely access a space we may have been systematically separated from, particularly those of us from big cities who live a day trip away from the coast. We may have to navigate stares and suspicion as we enter this less common environment. But always remember and walk with the knowing that most beaches are free for all to enjoy. It's a fine balance we've learned to gracefully pivot on. Has the trauma of racism clouded my judgement and made me overly cautious and suspicious? Or is it not just a trauma response, but from the behaviour of others and I'm picking up what they are putting down in real time?

We have over time made changes about fairness to our society by our presence, policy changes and the engaging power of our cultures, but work is still in process in smaller towns. Resurfaced prejudices aided by the fast-moving migration of young, diverse and middle-class families from cities to these coastline towns in a post-Covid world means, as before and right now, we're going to need to proudly rock those pride colours, and/or drape some Kente material on our chairs to brighten up the coastline and reclaim our spot.

Our presence in some spaces requires us to strip away colonial standards of beauty and how the 'normal' person is expected to present. Our music and food are forms of communion. The colours we bring are filled with energy that represents deities and nature. When we arrive at these beaches though, we can be arriving in worlds that have been whitewashed and stripped of these innate practises. People can be afraid of these differences, and fear can cause our bodies harm. Whether overtly or covertly.

Here are some considerations on beach access and tips on safety when navigating these spaces, especially in a non-conforming body.

Fishing as a Black or Global Majority Person

Coastal towns in colonial countries lack diversity and can be gatekept by rural, majority-white communities. Think Sydney, Australia where you would be hard pressed to see an indigenous person at the beach. Or hotels on the coastline of Jamaica that have privatized the beaches for holiday makers, which have unfortunately been allowed by the government to ban locals from using them.* Go back further and the current popular ideas on immigration completely fall apart. Black or Brown city folk moving to the coast in a WFH (working from home) era, or those conveniently considered "immigrants" isn't some new phenomenon but has been centuries in the making.

Over the years overt racism *has* become less common (although with the Trump presidency and the re-emergence of far-right ideologies

* https://www.jabbem.org/

in the UK it is dangerously moving backward), but micro-aggression is still part and parcel of moving through the world in a Black or Brown body. There are differences between how people of colour experience these microaggressions, but I have no desire to make this a teaching moment or retraumatize us. Our showing up on these coastlines is a loud visual statement as we change the face of fishing and acknowledge the more hidden histories of movements and contributions to these areas while reigniting our indigenous practices.

On enough occasions I've been told "Don't see many people like you fishing", that my staple reply – like a magician pulling the "card"– is "I see many like you. Must get a bit boring, init?" followed by a quintessential British pub laugh.

Look, these interactions don't happen all the time. Mostly, anglers are keen to strike up a fishing conversation with another passionate angler but, as we know, we carry the burden of getting too comfortable and then having that unexpected reminder shake up our day. If there's such a thing as balancing our openness and answer to being called to the wata with a little caution, let's use that finely tuned skill.

Beach Access and Signs

Don't assume you have an automatic right to always access any beach you choose. Fisherman's Beach in Hythe (a small UK military town), where we meet once a month for We Are Black Fish, is situated right next to a Ministry of Defence camp. When the red flag is up, you cannot pass that point as they are holding firing practice.

Make sure you check the security and warning signs when you get to a new beach. It may be mostly public but could also have restricted areas or times. Some don't allow BBQs or fires and ban dogs during the summer months.

Fishing as Neurodiverse

Being by the wata and fishing alone can be a great source of comfort for those who are neurodiverse and/or on the spectrum. The waves are great for regulating anxiety and the feeling of being so small amid a great natural expanse can make the world around quieter.

Here are some things you may want to consider before going fishing if you are neurodivergent yourself or going with someone who is or could be.

- How busy or popular a beach is and whether there are less busy zones
- Could the weather affect sensory sensitivities like temperature and sunlight?
- Consider taking sunnies to protect the eyes from too much sun glare
- Wear a hoodie to feel that extra sense of security against the elements.

Headphones can also be useful when outdoors for neurodiverse people, but I would refrain from using them while fishing alone, or try to keep at least one ear exposed. It's good to hear as much as you can around you. If you can hear the birds, they may be telling you where there is a shoal of fish you should jump at the chance of fishing. Also, if there are any beach announcements, you'll want to be able to hear them.

Fishing as Femme

Fishing as femme will draw attention. It can be a beautiful surprise for other femme people and inspire them to pick up a rod as well, which brings on the biggest smile, even while I'm writing this. But we don't all want, or always want, the attention, and it doesn't always arrive with good intentions.

Let someone know where you'll be that day and if you move spots. Find My iPhone or the Android equivalent can be useful too. I've got a personal alarm on my keys that is so loud, even the fish will come ashore if they hear it. You may want to use a pub or a cafe instead of a public restroom, as they are usually dotted along the beach promenade and have more people around. You can let them know you're fishing alone if queried. Or maybe use a female urination device if you know you'd rather stay at your chosen spot and don't want to leave your gear.

As previously mentioned, stay away from headphones and at least remove one earpiece. As a femme body you're safer keeping your head on a swivel and staying alert to your surroundings. I like that you can hear footsteps on a shingle beach. It's important to know when someone is walking behind or toward you, especially as your back is mostly to the beach and everyone else.

Fishing while Disabled

I spoke to Kyleigh Lough, Chief Executive from the Mae Murray Foundation to get better insight into the needs of disabled individuals in public spaces. What struck me first was the conversation around the use of the term "disabled people" using the social model of disability as opposed to the medical model "which believes that the person is not disabled; it's the environment that disables them and therefore the person has been disabled".

Fishing as only a sport and not a way of life can lend itself to this exclusionary thinking. We all need the resource that is the wata, for sustenance as well as mental, physical, and emotional health. The issues arise when beaches are not considered for all people and how they may show up, like being equipped with accessible changing rooms, beach mats and hoists. While it's important to advocate our local administration for "continued evaluation to be able to ensure that we can meet the needs of everybody" Kyleigh is aware that "It's not possible for every beach to be an inclusive beach", which is why it's important "to try and locate your activity at a location where the infrastructure is already in place".

This is how those of us who are not disabled can be allies to consider how others take part in fishing. "Our research really tells us that it's about taking part. And the taking part is what is most important, because that's not just looking on, that's actually being actively involved in whatever activity" for those that are disabled and groups who want to ensure as many people as possible can take part.

Fishing with Family or Chosen Family

Fishing and catching aren't always the only goal in mind. Sometimes it's the connection with people and the opportunity to throw in a day's fishing trip as a way of sharing skills, gear, bait and the travel cost. In a group, no doubt there will be someone who refuses to touch the worms, and no doubt there will be someone ready and willing to thread a worm on a hook and get stuck in.

Each one of our monthly hook-ups show me how much children love to hunt for whatever they are tasked to find or urged to discover along the beach. I've mass-collected flat rocks for soap holders and wood for the fire pit thanks to the enthusiasm of children. Something I'm less likely to do alone. If they're keen on fishing, get them a child-size rod to throw out there – they will be sure they have caught a big shark each time!

In groups, someone can be responsible for the pictures, especially if you're documenting your fishing journey. Or someone can chef the BBQ and food for your day out. If your group is diverse, remember your joy is an act of revolution and racial justice. Make some memories together and keep an eye on each other. And clean up after unuselves.

Other Anglers

I was in a session with two friends and their young son recently – three of us women, all queer and two of us women of colour. Whether this is a contributing factor to the interaction that ensued is hard to say for definite, but it was noted as a possibility. We started to unpack and set up our gear along the coast that other anglers had already lined up along. An older white man who was already set up to our left came over and started to speak to one of us – the only white woman in our group. Because we're in a group, I and the other friend went over to see what the conversation was about. You know, we had to check in. He doubled down on "informing" us that we should move further down the beach "cause as the tide starts running, we're all going to get tangled". He pointed down to where he suggested we set up and even shared that if we walked along the promenade it would be easier (we were on a shingle beach). For a moment, we debated about the distance away he suggested we move to – a good 15-minute walk – the tide and what it meant for it to run – and why something just didn't feel right. As we did, we realized that he himself was the same distance to the person next to him as we currently were to him. Wouldn't this mean he should also move? So, we carried on with our unpacking as he shook his head disappointedly because we chose to hear his "advice" and ignore it.

Look, the beach is a public space. He or someone else may very well prefer to have no one to the left or right of them, but that just isn't always an option. On a busy pier or marina, lines do get tangled with neighbouring anglers', and you work together to untangle them. You hold your rod up high, and they manoeuvre theirs under yours or vice versa. The day in question, not one of the lines got tangled during the session and he lived to fish another day. It's an example, if anything, to remember that the coastline is not the privilege of any one [type of] person. If there are a lot of anglers along the beach, be sensible and try not to get too close, and be mindful of the direction you cast out. Stay open, take on advice when it feels gentle on your soul and beneficial, give space when you can and reclaim your rightful place alongside those other anglers.

Safety Tips

Filming yourself while fishing is a great tool for learning, building a social media following and providing video evidence. People bring their troubles to the wata, and you may need to provide video evidence of incidents.

Size Limits and Fishing Sustainably

The laws around catching or releasing fish are murky waters. For people in Westernised countries, it can solely be a sport. You catch a "personal best" (a PB), take the pic, release it and buy a version of fish and chips on the way home to celebrate. For others, fishing is their income, and they generally take home what's put aside or not sold for themselves and their loved ones. For those of the global majority, fish and seafood are a food source and a cultural staple. The question of whether fish should be caught and released is based on the needs of their household. Now keep in mind, the average supermarket in the UK sells two small fillets of an overfished species like cod for £6. So that is what has been decided as OK by my government regulators who want us to keep buying from these stores.

Whether you catch or release a fish without interference from questionable legislators should be rooted in the innate understanding that *now* is the time *this* species migrates and is in abundance, so let nature provide. Simply looking at the fish will answer the question of whether it is too small to keep in my opinion.

Whenever I'm out during mackerel season, anglers keep fish of just about every size because "It's great bait for all year round", so the legislation on sizes and amounts we are told to abide by don't seem to apply then, because they are supporting their hobby. You see – murky.

The UK size limit for sea bass is 16.5 inches (42cm) but a lot of anglers would rather keep at least a 20.5-inch (52-cm) fish to bring home. Generally, those who make this choice are basing it on the fact that larger fish will make larger fillets, as they don't eat the whole fish. But eating the whole fish is what sustains people – and our oceans.

Fishing size limits are a microcosm for how the colonial mindset imposes rules on others, while simultaneously harming our planet. Colouring within the lines of governments and local regulations (that allow trawlers to destroy fish stocks and the ecosystem for profit, so supermarkets can sell two cod fillets) is about balancing your needs, the legitimacy of the legislation and your stewardship of the ocean.

For indigenous people who are from a lineage of farmers and anglers, fishing is not just a pastime, but it is a heritage, a culture and medicine for the body and soul. It's what has kept techniques for catching and preparing fish being handed down, letting each generation know they don't need to be tempted to buy every quick gadget fix. Or being sold food in constantly re-imagined forms. A spoon can scale a fish. A fish can be whole. In a time when presidents and prime ministers are creating separation through taxes and cost of living crises, looking back into practices like fishing as a way of living is becoming imperative.

Here's some practical wisdom I can share on size limits and fishing sustainably.

Tools for Recognizing and Measuring Fish

Each tackle shop that sells bait and fishing gear sells yearly tide time books. The first page of the one I always buy has pictures of fish found locally that help identify the species, and their associated size and catch limits. This is an important addition to your fishing bag, but this info can also be found online.

Cooler Boxers (or igloos)

These can often have fish rulers moulded into the top of them, which is great for measuring the fish right as you catch them. You can stick a ruler on them.

Catching and Eating Seasonally

Fish species migrate across the entire globe, just as winter provides us with root vegetables that warm us in the cold or summer provides green leafy vegetables that support the vitamin D and other nutrients we need in our bodies. Eating seasonally for the geographical location you live in is something humans did for millennia before everything was available all the time.

Search the Internet

Doing an internet search will let you know the latest fish size limits. Keep in mind though that some websites may not have been updated for many years, so will not give up-to-date information on how fish stocks rise and fall, so it's best to stick to your government's sites.

Tips When Fishing

If you're catching a lot of smaller fish and your plan was to catch fish for food, remember to stay present in the experience. Imagine fishing all day and not catching anything; at least you're catching. Each bite can look different, each reel feels different and each catch can surprise you. You're being given an opportunity to learn what's happening on the other side of the line. But if you'd rather fish for some dinner, then shift spots. Just moving a few hundred metres in either direction can land you in a school of something more desirable.

Lastly, collect up any old line, plastic and rubbish when you see it. The ocean has enough of a job to do without having to constantly spit back all we dump into it. It's a small act of sustainability that is a revolutionary deed of care.

Tying Your Knots

Tying knots is a constant practice that doesn't just start when you arrive at your chosen fishing spot, but before that, when you are home preparing for the next day. The night you just have that feeling that tomorrow will be fish on, so you choose your rigs and add your leader like the night before the first day of school when you laid your new shoes beside your bed, and they glistened up at you, ready for their big debut the following day.

Why Knots Are Important

Knowing at least one knot is crucial when fishing. You may have to connect your line to a swivel, or you may snap your line when casting if you cast out with the bail arm closed (which has happened to me a bag of times). You'll need to create a knot somewhere, when you restart the process of setting up your rig again. Remember to moisten the knot if you're using a monofilament fishing line to lessen the friction when tightening it – this way you don't create weak points.

Knots are also symbolic though, aren't they? They represent cycles, bonds and meeting points of not just pieces of 30-lb (13.6-kg) braid put together as a tool, but you and I and those in our lives put together. In those times the wata is like silk and there's a quietness that matches your inner peace, just as you sit back in your chair after casting, knowing something will happen soon. You'll get the chance to make a rig or prepare your lure rod by adding a leader line because those birds over there are interested in something as they circle or dive into a one condensed area. You can in the stillness of waiting and observing think about the knots created in your family lineage before you arrived as you sit in front a body of wata that we may have once crawled out of and stood up straight a million years ago. A reminder that the line and the knots formed didn't even start with you.

Online resources can describe step by step how to tie different knots. Videos are great as you can hit pause along the way to act out the steps yourself with some fishing line, and for those visual impaired have audio to follow along to. You can also find images for those that are visual learners. But rather than describe *how* to tie each knot, I want to speak about the knots I have found most useful for fishing as a metaphor for lineage.

- My Father – Palomar Knot
- My Father's Father - Albright Knot
- My Grandmother's Father – Loop Knot
- My Mother's Mother – Dropper Loop Knot
- My Mother – Blood Knot

My Father – Palomar Knot

My father taught me about the Palomar knot, although he was not an angler. He has never cast a rod and line, but he was skilled with a casting arm that could separate a father from a child. When he travelled from the Caribbean to an unfamiliar land – London, England – which should have been paved with opportunities for a decent living and at least a little sunshine, I suspect the knots in his stomach were as tight as a Palomar knot.

The day he arrived home from school to be told his mother had left for England and would "send for him soon" was maybe when he promised himself, he'd always tie his knots loosely. Without the experience of an angler, he didn't know that even if you tie a Palomar knot loosely, it will strengthen as more pressure is applied to it. I have in fact inherited the same tool of avoidance and know first-hand that when I've tried so much to ignore a thing, it has become an even tighter knot, keeping me closer and more connected to it. If only someone had shown him how to tie a Palomar knot, he may have understood its strength instead of fearing its connection.

Our knot has always been as strong and as loose as its design, as he would be out of sight for months or sometimes years at a time. By secondary school I had perfected the illusion of ignoring the knot firmly positioned in the pit of my stomach now until it bubbled with anger whenever my mother would, without fail, remind me of his approaching birthday each year, causing me to give the same eye roll response all teenagers have firmly in their arsenal. Consistency was learned from mother and clearly not my father.

I remember the day he met me after school to give me money for a coat. This was a rare occurrence. Meeting me. Buying something for me. It was a red coat I'd walked past many times on my way home from school – that bad boy red puffer coat in the shop window. How we managed to cross paths and be in the same place at the same time is part of the inexplicable life before mobile phones. It happened sometime between being afraid of bees after watching *My Girl* and thinking so much about girls, quietly and hidden, and the emergence of Jungle music in the 90's, where those thoughts were no longer hidden and, like a Jungle rave, not at all quiet. It was just the magic of the time.

He pulled up in a car I'd never seen. He smiled a smile I didn't recognize. His hair had a kink and coil pattern that made me wonder what it felt like to run a comb through it, as it looked softer and more loosely curled than mine, but closer in texture to mine than my mothers. I was wrapped up in the understanding that I got the easily-missed minutiae from him – even the kink and coil of my hair.

This is how I remember those random meetups with my father. I would, quite frankly, stare at the man, taking in the corners of his eyes, the slight stutter as he spoke. "He is absolutely my father," I would say to myself while nodding, like a detective known for having great instincts. But I could never quite see the heart or mind of the man and thus was sure even a DNA test to prove our relation like the talk shows did at the time would convince me. He handed me the £35 for the red puffer coat, and I smiled proudly to my friends "Yeah, that was my dad", all throwaway and teenager-like, because that day I had a father too.

The man who bought me the red puffer coat was the same man who taught me how to tie a Palomar knot before I ever fished. He taught me that just as a knot can be tied and untied, relationships too can be woven tightly or unravel if you don't follow the right steps. They can be a source of grounding through trust, patience and open communication, or they can come loose if when tied you let go of one end of the line. The Palomar knot – like the strands of DNA that gave me my hair's kink and coil, the shape of the corners of my eyes and my slight stutter – reminds me of our intertwined lives, even when we try so hard to ignore the stress and tension that's also being used to create it.

The Palomar knot is used to connect the fishing line to the hook because the line must pass through it, doubling up on itself to create a loop. The hook and hook eye need to be large enough, making it more difficult to achieve this with smaller and more common hook sizes. This knot makes me think about my father and how we have made attempts at reaching each other and how we've mostly given up as he and I just don't seem to fit. He would have to create more space or grow larger in some way, wide enough to hold me. But this knot, like all of them, is strong and it has been said that once mastered, you are able to do it with your eyes closed.

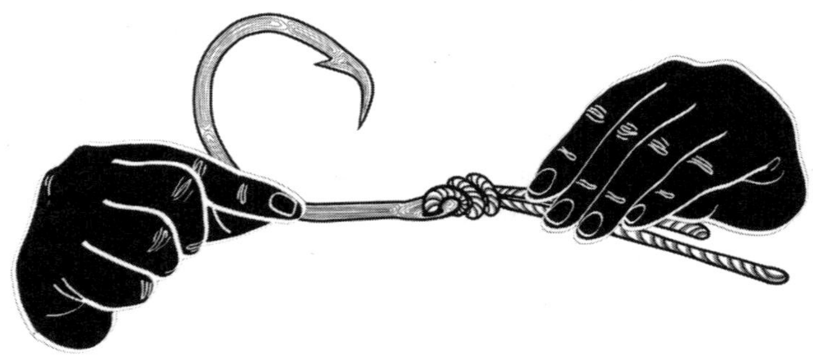

My Father's Father – Albright Knot

My father's father didn't speak much, just like the men I see sitting on fishing banks or shorelines, alone with their thoughts. He taught me about the Albright Knot although he wasn't an angler. As with the men on those banks, who possess a silent wisdom and know every kind of fishing knot, it's important to realize that it's a delicate and precise game of cat and mouse – or as the famous reggae song says "police and teef" – when engaging this solitary species. Want to know the best knot to tie when fishing for carp? Better be specific on the exact carp species one is referring to, the type of line being used and who scored the greatest inning in cricket, ever. These brooding figures to me represent an Albright knot, secure but requiring absolute precision or you could end up losing your catch.

When I see my father's father, I see someone moving backward. Not walking away, just not walking toward me. It's as if his thoughts and experiences are woven into his very being, his knowledge passed down through generations with very little conversation. One to many exchanges for him, and today's game of chit-chat is over. He may slip back into his focused meditation on the couch, the spot his body has chosen as its favourite resting place – always listening, but rarely ever making eye contact as he carefully loops his thoughts on the many conversations happening around him and having a lot on his mind, but usually too overwhelmed by the possibility of connection to share.

The Albright knot is used to tie two lines together. For example, if you are using a leader line, you'll use this knot to connect it to your main line. It's a great knot to know but I find it not so good on the go, while you're in a session. This is because of the steps needed: you have to create a loop with one line and then use the other to kind of wrap around it while also going back through the original loop and pulling steadily. It's a good knot for when you're at home though, and you have the time to give it a few goes. It's like the two separate lines can be tied together, which can be very useful, but they can just as easily come loose if not pulled to tighten in an exact speed and direction when they are being formed.

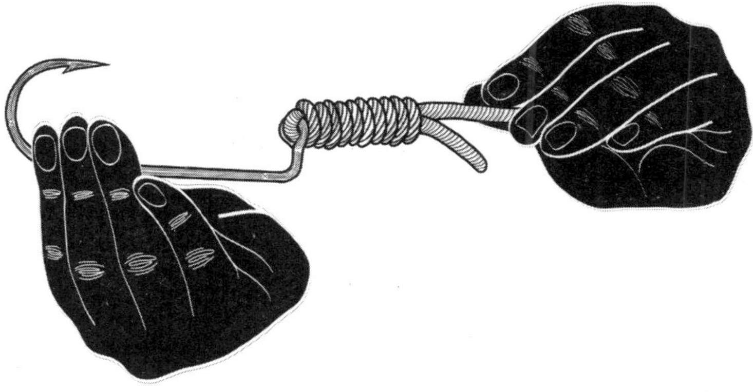

My Grandmother's Father – Loop Knot

My grandmother's father only materialized one day before I intended to commit a childish and rebellious crime. It was the dead of night, and I woke up from a deep sleep as if someone had called my name loudly. I shot up to a seated position and scanned the room. When visiting me, my maternal great-grandfather chose a seated position like my father's father and the men at the banks and shoreline. With his feet in the seat of the chair and his butt on the headrest, he stared at me with a look that can only be described as vex. I could make out the familiar crisscross pattern of the string vest wrapped around his chest, which was slim but athletic, like a farmer from the countryside. His elbows rested on his knees, and his eyebrows were thick and furrowed. This man was vex. As I started to make sense of his form, it occurred to me that he wasn't solid. It was as if a shadow had become 3D. The realization of what he was then hit me and I decided immediately that I would leave him be and mind my business by going back to sleep.

The next time I was at my grandmother's house, I described this incident. She made the sound that means everything, for every occasion: "Hmm." She left her workroom, rustled around in

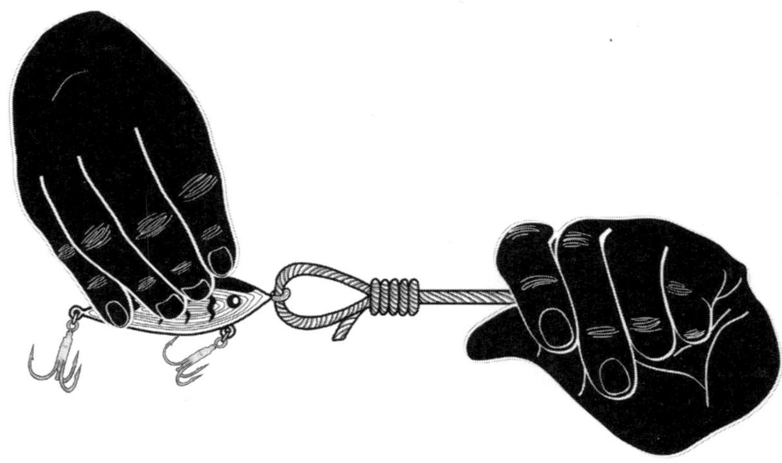

her bedroom, then came back with a picture that looked like an AI-generated image of a woman seated with a man standing next to her, hand on her shoulder. When I told her this was the man I had seen, her only words were, "He was a soldier in the war. Whatever you're doing, you better stop it." And that was that really. She understood his presence, and I was too stunned to question the validity, but smart enough not to tell her why I'd found myself face to face with an authoritarian ancestor. How is it that even without having a physical form or saying a word, my grandmother's father taught me a lesson? Like my father's father, who I only remember with small amounts of tentative eye contact, or like those men who sit on fishing banks and shorelines manage to teach me something about knots. There is sometimes a great distance between us although we are tied.

A loop knot is used to hold a weight or connection while it's being used and is then released again when you are done. It's a temporary attachment that allows for movement. When the weight or connection is no longer needed, it is designed to release and unravel cleanly like an ancestor who visits you in that space between being awake and asleep.

My Mother's Mother – Dropper Loop Knot

My mother's mother was a different kind of knot-maker, although she wasn't an angler. She had two distinct states of being. The first, wound tightly, with pursed lips and head down, focused on one of her five industrial-grade sewing machines, creating unbelievably detailed wedding gowns until the sun rose, cackling and talking back to her FM radio or her many grandchildren that bounced around her. Or the second, she was unravelling easily from anything or anyone who felt too close or too soft. Mumbling more than speaking to herself more than anyone. It would be unfair to call her a liar, but she did prefer telling tales that kept her most safe in her beliefs for most of my life. Until she began to grow much older, and wanted to release what was not her own story. Tales about how the white rum always present behind her bedroom cabinet was just to help keep the cold off her chest. Or that the men she had married were not actually based on her support needs or desires but, but rather the warnings of the older women who cautioned her that nothing would be worse than being unwed.

My mother's mother taught me to create art, grow vegetables from seedlings and to be confident in your talents. She taught me that the world needed artists and she was a living embodiment of dedicating your life to your art. But she also taught me that being an artist could well come before connection.

Here's what my gran taught me that I want to share. She left Jamaica by plane with one bag stuffed with what she could pick up and a child in gestation (my mother). This is a woman who learned to run to save her life. While she was in her later years, I started to record voice notes of conversations with her. Strangely for a woman who presented as stoic for much of her life, softly she told me stories that would interrupt my belief that my trauma was just my own. She ran from the man she married at an age too young to make such life choices but that was normal for the time, because he would drink too many drinks and become dangerous. On the last day of her life in the countryside of Mandeville, Manchester, Jamaica in 1958, her mother – my grandmother's mother – helped her pack a bag and got her to the airport on a flight to England before my grandfather realized what had happened.

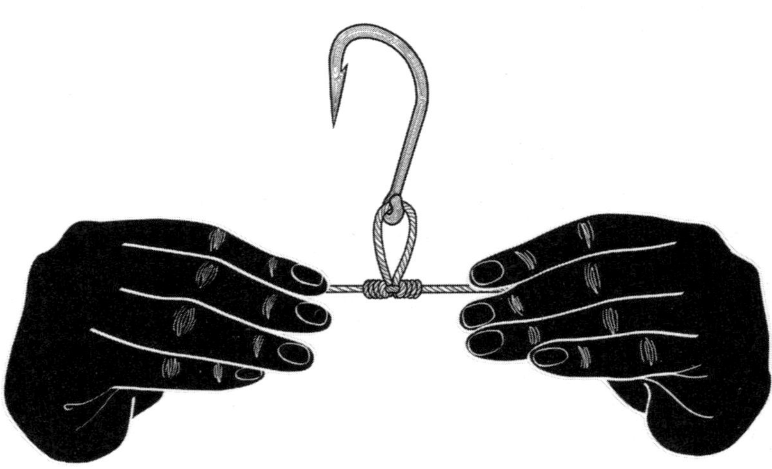

I come from a long lineage of women who have saved their own life the best way they know how whether that's to be quiet and keep the secret, to fight back in the moment, or to know when to run. To move. Forward, upward, anyhow.

A dropper loop knot is created when making a rig that can have multiple hooks but using only one piece of line, instead of connecting separate pieces of line. This means you can create a three-hook flapper rig with one long piece of line that is itself the rig. The ultimate survival rig when you need to make the most with what you have. Because it relies on itself and is spread thinner, it is known to have weak points that aren't obvious until one too many uses. The attachment points for the hooks can more easily tangle back onto the main line after some uses as well, as they are naturally being pulled back into their original shape, instead of being made of independent parts.

My Mother – Blood Knot

My mother held me so tightly that sometimes I felt I needed air. Her knots have always been the tightest: unyielding and secure. But my mother is not an angler.

These were knots tied with love and profound protectiveness. As I grew older, I began to question if these knots were also tied with fear – fear of letting go, of what could happen if I ventured too far, into the unknown. But in addition, without me understanding how she could hold these two seemingly conflicting things at the same time, she encouraged me to see the world. Her love is ineradicable, strong enough that you can sense it even when she isn't around. This meant that growing up, it could be suffocating. I had to learn to strike a balance between the safety of her bond and the freedom to explore and forge my own path.

I'm convinced that God, in whichever form you believe it to be, knew who my mother needed to be, for me. When I sit and make a rig, letting my hands show me what my mind can create, I'm reminded of who taught me to make what I needed without waiting for others to give me what they think I may need. My mother has always been a builder by nature. She was the one who connected those tongue and groove wooden floorboards with a hammer while Lovers' Groove music escaped the gold-trimmed, black stereo set. She put that duvet bed set together with an upper body strength kept secret from the outside world. My mother is the softest kind of woman, with edges that could cut through stone.

She has always been a catch! Walking through Brixton on a Saturday, shopping for my new shoes (her new shoes) was like dodging oncoming creatures in your favourite video game. The men's heads around us were on a constant swivel as she passed, vocal in their whistles and feral-ness. Her head, though, was always straight with just enough of a smile for them to feel acknowledged. I know why my father liked her, and I know why they were not meant to last.

The blood knot is my favourite knot because it is useful in just about all situations. It is a super strong knot that is used for tying your main line to swivels, rigs and connecting leaders. The need for this knot comes up in most sessions. If your line snaps, or you lose your rig or lure because it gets caught on something, you can use the blood knot to securely put those pieces back together again. Now this knot is the only one I'm aware of that is known for using at least five turns of the line around itself before the knot can begin to be created. This looping around itself is an embedding, an entwining and feels like a ritual as you count out loud, possibly the only time you hear your own voice on a solo fishing session.

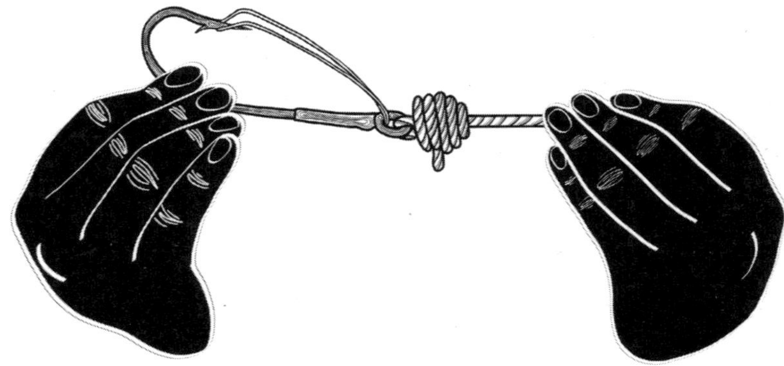

The Undoing

Like creating knots, untying the unintentional ones made from tangles and closeness in the quiet moments is like an act of meditation. You can see that just pulling at any end will simply make a knot worse. Tension and brute force are the enemy of undoing.

Taking the line back through the steps it took to become tangled is the best way to undo it. You've got to really pay attention to where it came from. Be led by the journey it took. Acknowledge without judgement the points of confusion that kinked and curled it on itself. There's a docility required in gently guiding the line back to where it started. But some knots, we have to admit, are unmanageable – such as braid used for its sensitivity that has rolled itself into oblivion. Making the decisions to cut and go is the best option. You've got fish to catch, baby.

Setting Up Your Gear

Imagine, it's the height of summer and you've got your chair and stand under each arm and your fishing rods in each hand. You've been contracted by your auntie to bring back two fish to fry up because it's a Friday and Fridays are otherwise known as Fish Friday where you're from. There are families to traverse with not one but two four-year-olds in the throes of coastline freedom. You're walking through groups of people to get a little further down the beach to claim a spot. There is someone's favourite beach blanket, a piece of colourful material that could have been some cushions – and still could be if the creative vibe kicks up on the right day – to avoid stepping on as you move past, Tetris- style. You can hear that one speaker, louder than the ones surrounding it, that has won the unspoken "beach day listening vibes" sound clash and is playing the type of house music that all sub-genre lovers are happy with. Or reggae, because who doesn't love reggae? So now all the people in that little microcosm, who have likely never met, have made a silent agreement and appointed their DJ for the day. And then there is you, who's reached far enough down the coastline that the music is more of an echo bouncing off the beach floor, giving it a natural delay and reverb.

It's important to remember that you've just walked through a culture, and culture is what feels like home. This is a space we share together. I don't believe that because we are anglers, we must leave our culture at home either. We should also bring it to the beach. The visual we get when thinking of an angler as a lone white man sitting on his army fatigue-patterned tackle box, green or black waders on, silent, waiting for a bite. But when we look at the world, it's *not* the norm when it comes to fishing as no such thing exists outside the construct. You rock up with your energy and vibe and bright orange tackle box like a ray of sunshine if that is the one the colour that appealed most to you.

When you've found your spot, here's a list of the gear you'll likely need, along with tips for setting it up.

The Rod and Rod Stand

Having unloaded my gear from both shoulders onto the ground, I usually start with the stand, if bait fishing. It's important to know when low and high tide are so you'll know where to first set up and can gauge whether you'll need to shift at some point during the tide change. Your rod stand should be facing the sea and, if need be, angled into the wind on windier days. Once your stand is erect, you can use it to rest your rods on, so both hands are free when setting up the rest of your gear.

Rods and Reels

Putting together my rod and reel is when the excitement really starts to build. I know this rod, I know this reel, and I know what we can achieve. Some things to remember:

- Make sure your reel is fixed on the rod with the bail arm facing toward the tip of the rod. This is the right way up.
- Loosen the drag so you can pull your line through with ease (but remember to tighten it again once the line is through).
- Make sure the line goes through each eye of the rod without being tangled or missing any eyes.
- Hold on to the end of the line once it's through the last eye and give yourself enough even line so that it doesn't fall back through when you let go. I can't even begin to explain the number of times I've threaded the line through each one only to let go and have it shimmy back through each eye at my expense.
- Knot quick link leader onto the end of the fishing line you've pulled though. I usually keep one on for a few fishing sessions, but some people like to tie a new one on each time. Your rig will then easily clip onto it, which makes changing rigs smooth and swift while fishing.
- In most rig set ups, your rig will have a swivel on one end (to connect to your line or quick link leader) and a crane swivel on the other end for your chosen weight.

Rigs

This is really about what you're choosing to fish this session. Each rig is best suited for different species. Even if you're aiming for one fish species, bring some additional rigs. You really can't say for sure what species is "on the feed". A super calming way of using your hands to create is by making your own rigs. There are boxes full of your average rig-making materials. When my uncle showed me how to make a two hook flapper rig that day it wasn't solely the rig-making that was the lasting memory, but he, my heart and life partner and I sitting at the kitchen table while he drank his coffee and balanced his smoke at the corner of his mouth, one generation to another, bonded in this passion we share.

Weights

For bait fishing you'll be using a weight. The size you'll require will be dependent on the wind speed. You need enough weight to cut through the wind, but make sure you check the side of your rod for the most weight it can handle.

Baits

The bait you use will be best suited to your geographical location. In tropical climates prawns and small live fish are common types of bait, whereas in the UK, worms and squid are more useful. You might prefer to use a baiting needle when using worms if you'd prefer not to be so hands-on. Prawns, worms and squid are threaded onto the hook (using the bait needle to help), so they lie in a way that looks as natural as possible. But saying that, I've seen people fishing with a handline made from fishing line, a hook and a plastic bottle with some fish guts in the end. It's really about using what's available to you.

Once you've cast out, smaller fish and crabs can nibble at your bait, which you'll notice as small taps on your rod tip. Although these fish are more difficult to hook and it's better to not respond by striking them (hooking them through the mouth), keep in mind that these smaller fish will attract larger fish. They are as interested as we are when slowing down to see "what happened here". Try and have more bait than you think you'll need to allow for more time spent in a session than expected or for experimenting.

There'll be times when a fish you didn't intend to keep swallows the hook and it will be more humane to dispatch it. If this happens and you're up for it, cut a fillet off and use it as "cut bait". But we'll look more at dispatching in the Fishing Chapter.

Lures

Keep a few lures on you for each session. If you have a light enough beach casting rod or you've purposely brought along a lure rod, then you may want to do some lure fishing in between your bait fishing. When fishing with my partner, she always brings a lure to break it up and change the energy from the more still and meditative bait fishing.

Pliers, Knife and Scissors

Have your pliers, knife and scissors within arm's reach. When the adrenaline is kicking in and you've got a fish you've just reeled in on the beach, you don't want to be rifling through your bags for these tools – especially since as you're going to be taking a picture or video of your catch first!

- You may need the pliers to help get the hook out of a fish's lip, particularly if it has teeth. Or if the hook has been swallowed by the fish instead of being mouth hooked.
- You'll use the knife if you choose to dispatch any fish you want to take home. A lot of people cut the gills off the fish after dispatching it to "bleed the fish" to give them a cleaner fillet with no blood lines for a cleaner taste.
- You'll use the scissors or knife to cut any line that may have become tangled and cutting it would be quicker than stopping to undo it.

Comfort Tools

I'm always shifting my chair around for the first few minutes after I cast out. I don't want it so close to the rod that my neck is angled up to sharply to observe any bites or movement. I may also be shifting to avoid looking directly at the sun. Being able to see the rod tip and move around your gear smoothly is key to a more chill session.

- *Days when I forget a tea towel pain my soul. You'll want to wipe your hands after touching bait, so make sure you always pack one.*
- *I try to wear a hoodie to block out peripheral view and focus. It's also a block from the wind or sun.*
- *Sometimes I like a little speaker, especially on a warm day or when I'm with friends.*
- *Bringing more than one layers of clothes is good because it lets you adapt according to the temperature and conditions. So, if it's warmer than expected you can take off a layer or if it's colder, put on an extra one. Especially in countries where the weather changes quickly.*
- *Waterproof clothing and boots for lure fishing is important as wet jeans or tracksuit bottoms will bring a deep sadness to the day otherwise pleasant day.*

Mindfulness Before Casting

In the moment after setting up and as you prepare to cast out, things will come up, such as a random to-do list item you forgot or recognizing you may have a little crick in your neck as you turn your head around to each compass point to check that niggle. Or questioning what those birds are doing and how the tide is moving to the left. Or how good it feels to be alone for a moment with yourself hearing only your own thoughts. Hearing your own heartbeat or the feelings of sadness that have been pushed down because you just haven't had the time. Does this moment allow you to feel like the favourite version of yourself? Or even just allow you to feel?

Here, by the wata, we're being given the chance to remember who we are on a soul level, away from the distractions. Like ancestors as old as Cheddar Man who've stood at the shoreline to feed themselves and their family and learn the land and sea that surrounds them. As they say in Jamaica, take a moment to "give tanks".

To follow are some reflections on mindfulness to consider as you step forward to the edge of the wata.

Your Nervous System

Once you've set up your rod(s), today's weapon of choice and connection to the sea and its secret life, pause for a second. Take it in. A smile might creep across your face because how *exciting* is this? How brave are you feeling? Reflect how in this moment you feel not weighted by the past, but alive in the present. Before you cast out, recognize this is the moment the research and passion come together to be expressed physically in one poetic motion. Breathe. Breathe deep into your belly.

Your Body

Consider what you've been carrying before you dropped that bag of gear off your shoulders to set up for the day. For me, it's often a reminder that I hold my shoulders too much, as though my body has agreed to stay alert and aware even though the need is no longer there. I like to say loudly (even in my head) "Lets 'ave it!" or clap as a reminder to make the energy move. Casting your rod out will be the act of joining the collective mission. Be grateful your body allows you to do this. How it has done what you have asked, many times. A privilege.

Your Thoughts

Doubt may creep in: "I'm not a professional. Who am I trying to impress?". That old script may come up, in that familiar voice that is not your own, wanting to know why *you* must be so different. In this act of fishing, you may be undoing decades of displacement from the wata and coastline and rewriting untrue social norms that say people like you don't fish. Or you may be reconnecting with the history of your own family or culture. Let it come up and let it come out and smile at being so "different" that you are choosing *yourself* in this moment. Notice both what you think about and what you are not thinking about.

Fishing is a comedy of errors, dressed up as a hobby, offered as a food source and source of joy, and observed/experienced as an absolute obsession. Embrace the chaos it brings. Be proud of taking a bag of gear unloaded onto a beach you may be visiting for the first time and managing to put the pieces together as well as J Dilla crafted just about any beat he touched.

You're not guaranteed to catch your chosen species or any fish on any given day. But you may get something larger than you expected or a species that wasn't even on your radar.

With that, now, let us fish.

THE FISHING

"Tight lines"

A FISHERMAN ON LAKE MALAWI

Photography taken by Alexis 2024

Casting

What Is Casting?

The act of casting out your line is poetry in motion. I say that with a fear of it reading as clichéd and cringe, but I can't better describe the elegance of this act. It is the point in which your entire body works synergistically. You're creating this kinetic energy as you enter a flow in which acts of faith become real, to catapult your hopes forward into the wata. As I try my best to describe the steps of casting your rod and line, try and imagine yourself doing so as you read. The imagination is powerful and acts as a safe and wholesome training ground. Like practising for your spoken exam, or work presentation in front of the imaginary crowd you'll no doubt wow the following day.

The action of casting (whether bait or lure fishing in a river, lake or canal) means to launch your baited hook or lure into the wata to reach those fish. This will allow you to position your bait past the shoreline (which can end up tangled in the power of the current unable to fish properly) or into a chosen area like a sandbar, reef or a flock of birds feeding on a shoal below the surface. When fishing on a boat though, the skipper may drift over a wreck or reef allowing you to drop your line into the deep without the need to cast, which is called bottom, or ground fishing.

With beach fishing, the distance you can cast, which will come with practice, acts as a clear marker between fishing larger baits on larger hooks further into the deep, and smaller and medium-sized fish closer to the shore. But it does not deliver those expected results each time. Casting just a few feet out can catch something big if larger species are hunting along the shoreline, particularly when its choppy. Remember, each cast can bring all kinds of treasures of species. Learning the art may seem like a rule, but like art, there are layers and factors that make fishing exponential in probabilities.

HOW TO CAST

First do your checks:

- *Is the reel securely attached to the rod? – Is the reel screwed onto the rod fully, as well as the arm of the reel tightened using the screw? I have lost the arm into the great blue as I didn't check it was tight and launched it along with the bait!*
- *Is that main line going from the reel correctly though each eye of the rod without missing any or being twisted?*
- *Is the leader and rig you may be using connected to your main line with a secure knot?*
- *Is each hook baited and secured with some bait string, if needed?*
- *Is the drag on your reel tightened? You may have loosened it to allow enough slack to pull the line through the rod eyes when setting up. If you cast with the drag loose, the line can cut your finger.*
- *Are the gripper weight's arms facing upward, making sure they can grip the seafloor?*

Firstly, position the rod over your dominant shoulder so the rod tip is furthest behind you. Once rested, open the bail arm of the reel while keeping your index finger of that dominant hand on the line (pressing the line onto the rod to hold it), wrapping the remaining fingers around the rod for grip. Your index finger will then prevent the line from being released until you let go.

Next, walk toward the wata's edge, checking there is no one or nothing your weighted line could encounter behind you for safety.

You now face the sea, with the rod armed on your shoulder, tip farthest away from you, your dominant hand on the rod holding the reel and index finger holding the line. With your less dominant hand, hold firmly near the base of the rod. So both hands are now holding the rod. This moment before you cast the line out is a chance to really connect with the rhythm of the wata and feel the wind direction. Between each wave that meets the shoreline, there's a calm as the wata pulls back into the sea. In this movement you may want to step forward to cast, so you're as close as you can get, before stepping back again after letting it swing. Wellies or wet boots will help you to avoid having to dancehall shuffle back to avoid getting your feet wet.

When you have decided the timing feels right, in a smooth but powerful motion, pull down on the rod with the less non-dominant hand while pushing forward with your dominant one. This downward and forward motion combined is the push needed to flick the rod's tip out into the horizon. You want to give it some welly here. You're sending that line, rig and weight out as far as you can. Don't be afraid of the power you have.

When the rod tip is just forward of being above your head, you *must* release your index finger (which is stopping the line). If you don't, the line won't be released and the weight will just swing down to the ground in front of you. Think of this as a 12-hour clock and you are standing in its centre. If 12 is above you, let go of the line at 2 or 10.

Now look, even after a decade of fishing, sometimes – often, actually – the cast doesn't go how I intended. I release my finger too late, and the weight gets sent straight into the shoreline in front of me with a whack, or many times, I've cast but forgotten to open the bail arm, which means the force I am using against the force of the bail arm's closed position snaps the weight and rig off, and my set up leaves for the sea as its final resting place. Saying that, I have collected set ups on the beach the following day when the tide goes back out and leaves it behind. The wata has a habit of regurgitating what it does not want to keep.

If the cast doesn't feel right, feel no way to reel it back in and try again. This is on your time. Just remember to go through the steps each time. Be OK with casting and not landing exactly where you expected, and then letting it stay where it is. It's not an act of trying to be right all the time. If a fish is passing by and it sees your bait, then that is how the catching will happen.

Lure Fishing

In terms of gear, you want a light lure rod and spinning reel combo. If using braid as your main line, connect a foot (30cm) or so of mono as your leader, to protect the braid from being cut by rocks or fish teeth as they launch at your lure.

The motion of casting with lure fishing is exactly the same as above. The difference being, once you've cast and your lure hits the wata, you immediately close the bail arm and start retrieving.

If you are lure fishing at the beach, try walking out onto more rocky areas or along the shoreline of the shingle and/or sand at low tide. This allows you to get closer to where the current is crashing against the rocks, causing more movement that releases oxygen bubbles and attracting fish. The latter means swells are running along the length of the shoreline, which predator fish use as hunting grounds.

Try a few different lures during your session to investigate what gets fish biting or following your lure in curiosity. With plastic lures, you cast them out and retrieve them by reeling the line back in steadily. Metal lures are usually heavier, so cast out, let the lure sink to the sea floor and then bounce it off the bottom in a jerking movement. This is done by retrieving it a little while pulling up on the rod, and then letting in sink again. Then repeating the process until the lure has been fully retrieved.

You can fish for mackerel by adding a rig with mackerel feathers and a small sinker weight on the end. Use the metal lure technique of sinking and retrieving.

Open Ocean or Deep Sea Fishing

For what's called bottom or ground fishing over the side of a boat, using a multiplier reel and casting rod combo is most common and easeful as you may be holding your rod a lot of the time instead of resting it on a stand. Fish are going to be larger in these deeper watas, so make sure you've prepared for this trip by using a stronger main line (30lb +), with a strong leader line and larger hook set up. Flapper rigs are good when baited with small bits of squid on each hook for a shoal of fish, while a whole squid on a larger hook is great for larger solo species along reefs or in wrecks. Plastic lures are also used when fishing over wrecks with a boom rig that allows the lure to float far enough away from the weight so as not to get tangled while it sinks and is retrieved through this deeper wata.

Wind Speed and Casting

The wind gust speed and direction will make a difference to the weight you'll need and the casting direction. With stronger winds you'll notice your weight doesn't quite cut through the air and move forward enough. In this case, switch your weight up for something heavier. But don't go over the weight limit your rod allows, which will be in the packaging and/or written on the rod itself. When there's less wind speed, you can go lighter.

If there aren't many other anglers or people swimming, try using a rolling or bomb weight instead of a gripper weight. This allows the bait to gently move along the sea floor, widening your fishing area.

Now wind direction is the thing of legend and superstition to the seasoned angler and novice alike. When I'm driving and need to ask for directions, and the response starts with compass talk (N, S, E or W), I immediately throw the towel in. I just nod and smile, hearing and registering nothing. This is *not* the language of my gentle heart. Saying that, it is good to note the direction on the days you catch more or less, to better understand any correlation. The saying amongst anglers is '**Wind from the west, fish bite the best; Wind from the east, fish bite the least'.** This is to do with the rising and dropping in pressure that is associated with each direction.

Apps will let you know the direction of the winds and the currents, and even the likelihood of fishing under those conditions. But keep in mind your body and senses will tell you a lot more the more you practise. Work with nature, not in opposition to it. Shift your stand so your rod and line are facing the same direction as the wind so the set-up is not being pushed. The same way a pet at home will keep readjusting itself to stay in the sun being cast into the living room, pay attention to what feels most comfortable and makes most sense.

Casting Direction

Think about *where* you are casting. Fisherman's Beach in Hythe, where we have our monthly hook ups, is a working commercial fishing beach. There are boats beached directly on the shore that go in and out daily. Using a pulley system, with huge round wheels dripping with decades worth of oil, to keep them rust free and smooth in any weather, the boats are winched up on the skippers' return from the sea. A few hundred metres out in the sea is a brightly coloured buoy that the boats are also tied to in case the pulley system ever fails or the sea rises so high in a storm that it moves the boats from where they are stationed. The pulley system is holding the boat on one end on higher ground, and the rope connected to the buoy is holding it on the other in the sea. If you were to cast across that rope, you would probably (unless very lucky) get your hook(s) caught on it, and would have to cut your line, saying goodbye to your rig and weight. Always check what's around and take note of areas where you've got caught before.

If you're fishing with two rods, think about where you want both casts to land. Will one be closer and one further out? Will one need to be cast more to the left or right, allowing for the movement of the current, so the two lines do not cross each other?

Same Movie, Different Cast

I learned to cast out a line long before I fished, the act itself being an act of faith.

Many moons ago, at the age of about 14, I wanted to be a singer. This was to be one of those casts where you forget to open the bail arm and you snap your line. My singing dreams were cut just as short as these casts, when I bravely gave a rendition of whatever "Brandy" song we were all obsessed with at the time. As I pushed the air from my timid and hopeful chest, my vocal cords squeezed in a way that meant the air and subsequent sound escaping was as unnatural and disconcerting enough to let myself, and those around, know this would not be my contribution to the world.

But I was called to use my voice in some way and had been secretly practising the art of rapping along to music videos and the behest and humour of my mother most likely – a natural progression from my love of poetry at the age of nine. There was a rapper called Da Brat who was the first masculine identifying woman I had seen so comfortable and accepted in her skin. She was skilled and she was proud and she had a huge impact on me. Then on one of those days listening to late night radio (when hip hop was exclusively played in the UK) I heard the single "Slippin'" by DMX. The poetry, the pain and the hope spoke to my spirit, on the edge of me. The hairs on my arms stood up and I inhaled deeply.

On the way home from school on the back of a double decker bus in south London not long after, while the boys showcased their raps to each other and, but mostly to us (the girls), one of my friends exclaimed, pointing in my direction, that I could also rap, as heads spun toward me in doubtful unison. On the spot, with nowhere else to go, I did a four-bar rap, which was as much as I had written by that point in my career, and the bus erupted in shock at the girl who could rap in a time when "girls don't rap". They were impressed this time, and I knew it. In that moment I was hooked – being seen on my own terms. Eyes on me because I wanted them there.

Fast forward to around the age of 24/25 and I'm working on making music with an old friend, in his home studio, where his mum didn't seem to mind the repetitive kick drum on loop and the self-taught midi keyboard melodies filling the space. He and I together were good food. Some people you create with feel like you meet in an ethereal place where you're able to grab ideas like those cash machine games on Saturday night TV shows, where one lucky winner gets to keep all that they can grab as the perfect team. I'd heard Me'shelle Ndegeocello's album *Bitter* and was inspired to make an album that was as orchestral and moving, but hip hop. I loved the strings, the softness and smoothness of its gentle power.

During one of our bi-weekly studio sessions, I asked my friend for a copy of the Yellow Pages. If you know what that is, hello old friend! This *Lord of the Rings*-type relic of a book contained the contact details of every business in the city, town or local area, including record labels. I looked through it and found one I like the name of.

Now this wasn't my first time being in contact with a record label. I previously did a verse on *another* friend, NATS', album. A young intern at the time who heard my verse got in touch and a meeting was arranged. It didn't go badly, but it didn't go, well. In those days – a Black girl who rapped was rarely allowed space in the UK charts as we are more commonly now. I was told after the label team listened to my demo that, if I "could sing too", they might be able to make this happen. Singing – my old nemesis. This was not wata I cast into and felt comfortable in at all. So, I stayed in my lane. That label's early days of being the "urban department" situated a tiny back office of a much larger building turned into a major force a decade later. Powerful enough to drop the word "urban", as Black girls like me took up their rightful space in the charts.

Back to my friend's home studio where I see the label with the name I like, so I call them up with my £5 mobile phone credit. After a few rings a guy answers and I give him the spiel of me being a rapper and that my friend and I are making these songs, like orchestral, but hip hop. He responds frankly, "I like the tone of your voice. Can you come and see me now?' I say yes before I even know who he is or where seeing him would take place. He gives me the address and we hang up. My friend is willing me to update him immediately, with his wide eyes and posturing. When I show him the address I was given, he looks at it, tilts his head to one side to let the words bounce across his mind, and says "But this is my street. This is the street we're on"! Is this a sign of madness? (Not uncommon to me.) Is this the same street as the home studio is on? Considering I was there so often, I at that point realized I had no idea of the street name. Is this man I don't know somehow conspiring with imaginary forces to play a wicked and cruel trick on me? Or was the random number I called a record label that was based a few hundred metres down the road from where we had been making music for the past six or seven months?

As you can imagine, I went to that meeting. My friend deciding to stay and wait for the update – new people and places were not his ministry. He was a producer of energy but tentative with his own. In fairness he was probably feeling the weight of this out-of-worldly coincidence. If I could have felt much at that time of my life, I would have felt it too. That day I played the head A&R (who I later found out never answers the phone) three tracks. He listened to them all on that Friday and offered me record deal the following Monday. One of those three tracks "finish the album" made it to my debut album *Speech Therapy,* released 1 June 2009 and went on to win Album of the Year at The Mercury Music Prize, becoming the first rap album to do so.

I learned to cast out a line, long before I fished. In wanting to be seen on *my* terms, I had practised sending my hopes and dreams into unknown watas ever since I felt the magic of those four bars in the back of the bus.

To be fair, I had cast out a line before that, and even when it landed like a bomb in front of me, I cast out again. Have you considered and offered softness to yourself for the times you have done the same?

There's something important about casting your line into the wata, baited, or lured, but set up by you. There's an empowerment that comes with taking your own chances in the vastness. There may be the hook of a bite, the tiniest fish you've ever seen, or a Thornback ray with a wing space that makes it look like something from outer space. You may even spend the best part of ten minutes pulling in a rock from the seafloor that you hooked unknowingly. It happens, trust me. But each time, you'll want to cast your line back out and see what you can hook next.

But back to casting ...

Setting the Line

You've now sent your line out into the sea and your weight has hit the surface. The connection has been made. At this stage you want to set your line. This process is to make sure there is no slack when it's resting and fishing, so that you can better see a bite.

Once that weight has broken the surface, it's very quickly going to hit the seafloor especially at the beach. After waiting just a few seconds, without closing the bail arm, hold the line softly against the rod. You're now going to walk your rod back to the stand for it to rest and wait for the bang!

As you walk back, you'll start to feel the point of tension being created in the line after a few steps. At that point, let out a little line, but not too much. Then hold onto the line gentle again. Remember, it's about keeping that point of tension, not pulling past it. Every few steps, repeat the process of letting a little line go when you feel the tension.

It's weird, but this resistance you get with the tension, knowing the weight is now holding itself on the seafloor, is like having a teammate out there. It makes me think of those spearfishermen in the deep, with boats patiently waiting each time they resurface to make sure they do resurface and receive any treasures. It's your secure anchor that you cannot see but know is there.

Once you're at your stand, place the rod down and close the bail arm. Give the reel a gentle wind to retrieve any slack. You want to see a little bend in your rod tip appear.

Every so often, especially in stronger currents, create a habit of turning the reel a little, to regain that point of tension as the sea's power causes slack incrementally.

Recasting

If you cast out and it goes wayward for any reason, fight the urge to automatically reel it back. Go with it. The little voice in my head that shouts "Shameeee", like a classroom of 12-year-olds in perfect chorus, is *only* in my head. I'm still learning to quieten that voice and act like I know that nobody is watching or equally invested. But *I* am. And somewhere in between that icky feeling and ultimate reality is a place of contentment in being more like the wata and going with the flow.

Sometimes a session with a lot of catches, or say on shingle beach at low tide where you must cast at the shoreline then walk back over the mound of shingles each time to rest the rods, can be a tiring. In those instances when a cast doesn't land where I had intended, I'll absolutely leave it. There it landed and there it will fish for now. Again, a shorter cast does not lessen your chances of catching. The aim is to be a part of the process; have your line and hook in the mix. If the fish wants to take a bite, it will do so wherever it is in the wata.

If you notice once you've set your line that it has drifted dramatically to the left or right, make the decision based on who or what's around on whether a heavier weight is needed to secure the set up. You probably should recast sooner rather than later in this instance.

Here are some other reasons you may need or want to recast:

Checking Your Bait

You should bring your line in after every 15 minutes or so to check it. You might check your bait and the hook is as naked as the day it arrived in the post. And this is without seeing a clear bite once. This is why it's good to have more bait than you think you'll need. If this happens, switch to smaller hooks, as small fish are likely nibbling away at your bait around the hook, instead of swallowing it.

Checking the bait and then deciding what to do next is your chance to read the information this session is giving to you. Cast again in the same place, or try a little to the left, or right this time? Cast out further, or closer? What's the tide line like – time to shuffle your gear, or stay where you are?

Clearing

Using two rods means the lines can get crossed, as does fishing with a friend who also has a line or two out, or other anglers either side of you. This happens when fishing on a boat a lot as you are often drifting along with the current among up to nine other anglers. If you get tangled on your own lines, bring them all in and place them on your rod holder to free up your hands, allowing you to untangle. If tied up with someone else's line, encourage them if they are not doing so already to bring in their line as well for the same reason. Untangling on land is where we do this work best.

During the change of season in the northern hemisphere around late spring into summer the wata begins to warm, causing a phenomenon named "May Rot". When this happens, microscopic plant-like organisms called phytoplankton are released, which releases a foam-like scum. It's been said by some anglers that the fish are less active at this time because the May Rot irritates their gills. Others are not such strong believers in this. But I do know that the foam gets stuck to your line as you can see it as you're retrieving. Try a whipping motion of your rod to shake it off, or pull it off by hand. It's always a good idea to rinse your rod and reel after saltwater fishing as salt erodes, and even more so during this season.

May Rot can also lead to an accumulation of toxins in shellfish like mussels, which are fixed to one structure, so avoid foraging as a food source in this time. The old age advice is to only eat during months than have an R in them, even if you're going to cook them, because this does not kill the bacteria. They are fine as bait all year round though.

When Lure Fishing

When lure fishing, metal weights are heavier so they can reach the sea floor and be retrieved in a twitch motion imitating an injured fish. Top lures are lighter and designed to be retrieved quickly because they imitate a fish dashing away from trouble along the top. These different styles of lure require a different retrieve technique, so it's worth trying as many styles as you can every few retrieves. Switching lures while in a session will give you not only practice in technique but also allow you to fish in the different depths of the wata to investigate what's around. This makes lure fishing the ultimate practice in recasting.

Waiting

Once I've cast out, set the rod(s) to in their resting place, and tightened the line removing the slack, I first want to sit. Ground myself. An exclamation sound escapes my mouth like the auntie that I am, feeling proud of my set up and my courage to invest in a practice that ignites and slightly terrifies me as I finally make my way back to the wata and back to *me*.

When I sit still in my fold-up chair, even for just a few minutes, not needing to be anywhere but where I am, I question (knowing the answer) with a smile, whether it even matters if I catch any fish today.

Waiting isn't a passive activity. Stillness is not "doing nothing".

We experience time differently, depending on the energy we're holding. When it's been more minutes than you'd like without a bite (often your first cast is like that as the scent of your bait hasn't had time to attract fish) and your blink rate goes up because maybe it's your eyes that just aren't seeing the bites (it's not), and your head has been on enough of a swivel that you're concerned you might now just be staring at people doing things that don't concern you, it can feel like a long ting. Have you tried meditation? I'm talking feet criss-cross, hands on knees, palms up meditation. I can't tell you how I've struggled with this over the years. Whatever is meant to happen always takes too long to happen for me. These moments while waiting for a bite are my act of meditation though. If you've also struggled with the conventional forms, invite yourself to see how this feels.

Bird Activity

The best visual indication you'll get for when fish are around in large numbers, are from the watchers in the sky. With their vantage point and accurate eyesight, they can see what's happening under the surface from miles away. If you're beach fishing and you see a group of birds squawking and diving, there is a 100 per cent chance there are a lot of fish right there. In fact, it's probably a feeding frenzy. During the summer months in the UK, when anglers pick up their mackerel feathers to fish into the huge shoals of mackerel, you can see small fish such as sardines being chased so close to the shoreline that they can be collected by hand. They make a tasty snack, if still alive, and good bait if not. If you have a lure rod with you, jump into action with both feet and go crazy. The sounds, the visuals, the heartbeat – it will be magic. If you don't have a lure rod, then recast into the direction of the frenzy with your beach set up and watch that rod bounce.

Enjoy Yourself a ~~Little~~ Lot

A sunny day is glorious for the vibes. It's the type of session you will likely do for the feel-good factor as much as for the fishing, especially if you are with your chosen people. Not long ago I fished with a friend whose friendship has been formed through moving to the coast and she, her partner and four sons attending the Hook Ups. Since that first session they have become like family: queer, mixed heritage and finding themselves and new joys in the art of fishing. We had one of those out-of-office days (this friend has been training to be a captain to eventually teach fishing to our participants) where we link up with our two rods, stands, fresh bait and croissants for the coffee. When I tell you, we talked. The sun was blazing, the wata had just the slightest of heartbeats, and with my chest full of words I couldn't quiet they spilled out like a stream of consciousness. She nodded and listened and held space and then shared that her chest also gets too full of words she can't always form. Every time we checked the bait the hooks were empty, as we missed each bite. That day we fed fish freshly dug up lugworm instead of catching, and that's ok. Sometimes the fishing isn't fishing, it's therapy.

Remember that the sun will dehydrate you, so keep fluids up. Bring a little fruit or something that can be eaten from its natural or plastic jacket, so you don't have to touch with your hands, which might be a little mucky.

Send the voice note to your friend you've been meaning to show you've been thinking of. Check your socials. Snap some pics. Make a perfect fishing playlist. Take care of yourself.

Move Your Body

Don't be afraid to move around a little. I'm London born and bred, and we learn fast in the city to make sure everything we love most (our phone) is right where we can see or feel it at all times. Are you from a city that teaches you to keep your head on a swivel and an eye on everyone? Try and soften a little here at the wata's edge. There is only the tiniest of likelihood that someone will arrive randomly, pack up your gear and lug it off the beach in a slow meander while you wander a short distance.

The wata itself is teaching you that it takes what it wants, and even then, you might get it back at low tide. At worst, things can be replaced. But your time spent on a little walk discovering the patterns in rocks painted over time and compression, allowing the child in you to discover new sights, can't be. Your time is as precious as you are.

Make Notes

You may notice if fishing in the UK that the best days of weather on our skin aren't the best for fishing. Very UK-coded. As though that calm wata that comes from little to no breeze as the sun is blazing without interruption in the sky has the fish doing their own version of a relaxed beach day on the seafloor. Hardly moving, not biting. Have you noticed that this is your third session at this spot, and you look around and yet again all other anglers seem to be fishing a different part of the beach than you, which seems to correlate with your loss of lures gulped by hidden structures or rocks? Did you just go through three months of catching flat fish and suddenly they change to a more colourful and fast-moving species? Could this be about the change in season or the migration? Do you need to try a different size hook now to match the change? Noting down observations will help you start refining your sessions.

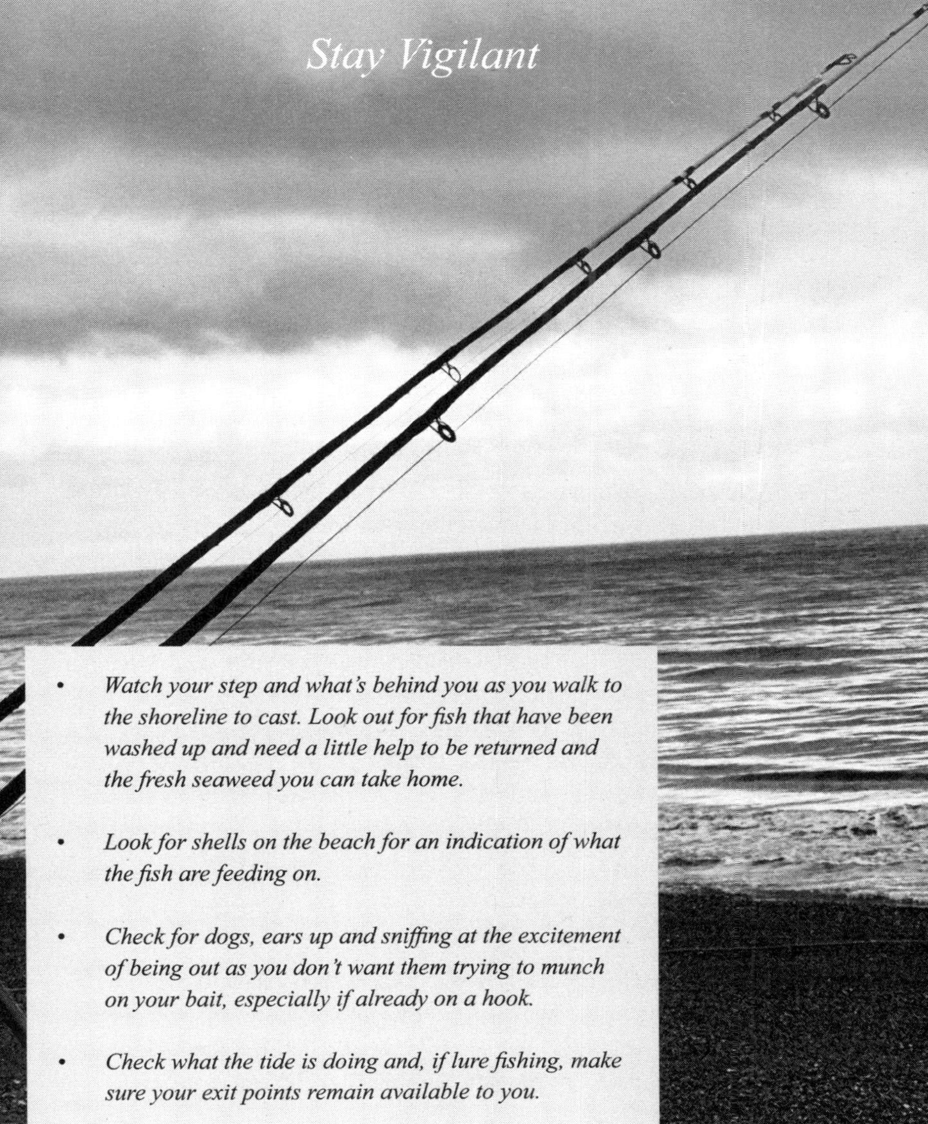

Stay Vigilant

- *Watch your step and what's behind you as you walk to the shoreline to cast. Look out for fish that have been washed up and need a little help to be returned and the fresh seaweed you can take home.*
- *Look for shells on the beach for an indication of what the fish are feeding on.*
- *Check for dogs, ears up and sniffing at the excitement of being out as you don't want them trying to munch on your bait, especially if already on a hook.*
- *Check what the tide is doing and, if lure fishing, make sure your exit points remain available to you.*
- *If you want or need to move away from your set up when you have a line out already, then loosen the drag slightly. This means if you do get a bite from something big it will pull the line and not your whole rod, stand and God knows what else. Fish are strong – we'll talk about that in the next chapter.*

Fishing for Bait

If you have a smaller set up on you like a 3,000-spin reel and bass lure rod, add some sabiki feathers (very small hooks) and try fishing for your bait. Drop the line over the side of a pier, warren or estuary, or cast out into the shoreline and let it hit the seabed with a sinker or a rolling weight. Once that lead hits the floor, then just bounce it up and down the column or, if at the beach, use the pull motion of mackerel fishing, while steadily retrieving it back to you.

You'll want a live bait rig with a single large hook and rolling weight ideally ready to go. It's good to have a little bucket with some sea wata to put the fish you catch in immediately. Small fish especially don't last very long out of the wata. You can leave them in bucket while you continue fishing for more. Take your caught bait fish and push the hook through its mouth with the tip facing upward. Then either drop it back down or cast out again.

Fishing with live bait means a predator fish will strike, not just investigate with a nibble. So be prepared for the action to happen. The best way to do this is to remember to loosen your drag a little and be ready to respond to the line being pulled and the sound all anglers love of the line being pulled from the reel as a big fish whizzes away. You can also use smaller fish you catch, but not alive, hooked onto a two hook flapper for example. Or keep in the freezer for a future session.

Undoing Those Knots

You'll spend a lot of time untangling knots. You may retrieve your rig and find that both the hooks on your two-hook flapper rig have met and tangoed themselves into a spin. Having additional rigs as well as using a quick leader means you can simply unclip and replace it.

When presented with a tangle, before you start moving any parts around, remember that tension is the enemy of undoing. It takes care to unravel well, so approach it with patience.

Focus on one area, or one hook at a time, and trace the line back through the steps that led to the tangled mess. Acknowledge the journey and exact points of confusion that led to the formation it found itself in. Now you can just put it to the side for later and never get to it or you can throw it away. But in doing so, you may miss the opportunity to reflect to yourself that everything that can get itself into a mess deserves care and patience to be undone. If the knot is just too much to handle, give yourself grace and cut it. Knowing when to cut your losses is equally important.

Patience and Persistence

In the early days of fishing, you'll just be mostly trying to remember the steps. Everything can be frustrating in this stage of the process. A number of times I set up my rod and reel only to realize I hadn't made sure the line was going under and over the bail arm of the reel, so nothing happened when I engaged it and went to retrieve it. Or that I missed an eye on the rod when threading the line through. But it gets better. Once you've learned the steps they become second nature, which frees up your mind for taking in the information your surroundings and the session are offering so you can get creative. The creativity, inspired by the need, is what got us humans to fishing in the earliest times in the first place.

Bite Indication

What Is a Bite?

This is it. The location prep, the gear on the shoulder that you dropped at the spot your feet said stop and your spirit said: here. You've baited up, cast out and entered your rightful ticket in the prize draw. You've had the time to watch and see the tide, the birds, what's around. You gave a nod to the neighbouring angler, the head tilt that says, me too – good luck – tight lines. You got a chance to appreciate the clean air, the lapping waves, the beauty of the whole experience as one song perfectly equalized so the bass feels like someone humming with no rattle or distortion. You're sitting, baiting up a pennel rig of some squid wrapped around a few lug worms and tightly bound with bait string, then you get a bite … and this is the bass drop that sends everyone's hand into the air in unison. A bite is letting you know something is at least investigating your bait or lure, if not picking that bad boy up like a street taco on the back of a motorbike and is heading home with their newfound feast. But before we can strike and hook this fish, we need to understand what a bite indication is.

We can break it down in the following way: a bite is when a fish is interacting with your bait and the signal of this is being sent through your line and your rod. The fish pulls the hook to swallow the bait and because of the tension you created this pulls or vibrates your line as the energy travels through it.

What to Look Out for?

The Nibble

Imagine this like a tentative knock on the door: soft, but clear enough to indicate someone is there. These light vibrations could either be a smaller fish nibbling away at your bait not affected by the hook and instead eating around it, or something like a crab using its larger claw to hold the bait and its smaller claw to cut through it.

Flat fish bites can look like a nibble, though. If you are fishing in their season or where it's been known they are currently located, then look out for nibbles that have a slight tremble to them. This happens when flat fish move their bodies on top of the bait to eat it.

The Knock

These are a build-up on the nibble. The rod tip will look like it's being pulled down in quick succession, like an old school door knocker. It's solid, and more obvious than a nibble. It means a fish has the bait and hook in its mouth.

The Pull

This is an undeniable bite indication. Your bait is in the fish's mouth and on the move with enough force that the weight holding on the seafloor has been lifted, making the rod tip bend down toward the ground. It's likely already hooked itself, but this is less guaranteed without striking. We'll get into striking in the next chapter.

If the drag on your reel is tight (which is very possible if you didn't plan on catching a big fish) then you need to move fast and grab your rod, as it could not only knock your gear over, but pull the rod in completely.

Slack Line

If you first see a pull and then the rod tip immediately retracts into a completely upright position (without the tension curve) the fish has taken the bait and hook into its mouth and lifted the weight on the move, but instead of swimming away from you, is swimming directly towards you. React in the same way as above by picking up your rod, ready to strike.

How Conditions Affect Bite Indication

Wind Speed

On calmer days you'll see less movement in your rod. If you don't feel the breeze, the rod won't either. If it's a little windier, the rod tip may shake a little from left to right. This is different from the up and down pull of a nibble, knock or pull.

The Current

When there is a tide, there will be more movement. It's likely you'll get more sway in the rod tip up and down. This is because the line itself is being pulled and released by the waves. The easiest way to differentiate between the tide and a bite is by making the visual connection between when the tide rises, and the rods movement. The tide will create a smoother up and down motion, and in unison with its movement.
Fish bites are non-rhythmic. They will completely break the rhythm of the tide. You're looking for 1, 2, 3 knock, or a pull or a nibble that looks like rattling or vibrating. Having two rods in a session helps as you'll see the wave pull on both, either simultaneously or one after the

other depending on where you have cast each line. If the movement is happening to both, it's unlikely to be a double bite – unless a shoal is passing and, in that case, you'll get to breathe again when it's all over!

Night Fishing

When night fishing, use a luminous light that clips on the rod tip. It really shows you what's happening in the dark. Now night fishing will mean that larger fish are out on the hunt, so you'll be getting knocks and pulls. Remember to loosen your drag if targeting larger fish with larger baits. Even if you don't see the bite, you'll hear the famous whizz of the line being pulled from the reel. This is called a "run".

How to Prepare for Bite Indication

The Line

Braid is more sensitive than mono so, if you use this, you'll be able to see the smallest of bites better, especially when shore fishing and you're not holding the rod and will be relying on the rod tip's movement.

Drag

Remember to use a tight drag for smaller to average fish so you can better see the nibbles and knocks because of the tension, and looser drag for bigger fish so you can let them pull and then run.

If you're fishing with two rods, try using one set up with a two- or three-hook flapper rig for smaller fish (which doesn't mean you won't catch bigger ones), with the drag set tight to detect those nibbles and knocks. The other rod can have a larger bait on a rig like a pulley pennel cast out as far as you can, with a looser drag. This means even if there is more action on the smaller set up keeping you busy, you'll hear the run of the other without having to keep eyes on it as much.

Lure and boat fishing bites

Now with lure fishing or when fishing on a boat while holding your rod, the energy of the bite will be directly transferred to your hands. This could happen as you cast out over the side and your bait or lure starts to sink, or as you're retrieving the line back to the top, or back to you. The bite can happen at any point and honestly there is nothing more incredible than to be deep in convo or having a random thought and be yanked back into this reality when you feel that pull.

If a fish has seen your lure and is chasing it, you might first experience a tapping sensation as it lunges for it and misses. This is the moment to be prepared for a bite and slow down your retrieve some. On a boat, you will feel a tug (or succession of tugs) or solid weight on your line.

With both, keep an eye on the rod tip as you would with beach fishing. I may be distracted for a moment and feel a tug or tap that draws my attention back to the rod. Looking at the rod tip and seeing it pull or knock at the same time as feeling it confirms any suspicions of fish taking a bite.

Bite Uncertainty

Stay curious and don't feel like you shouldn't be too excited. React to what your instincts tell you to. Is it a bite? Can you be sure? Not really. You may be on your own fishing, learning, trying or with others who are learning and trying too. Even the most experienced of anglers are forever learning and trying. Remember that you do not have be sure, you just have be present and paying attention to respond to what seems like a bite – the willing participant you already are.

It's like stepping onto a stage, nerves flooding your body with adrenaline as you are handed the microphone and the host asks "For one million pounds, is that a nibble or a knock?" Don't doubt yourself or be afraid to say, "Today I don't know, but I'm about to find out". And clap for yourself.

Nina Simone was asked in an interview what freedom was to her. Her response has stuck with me. After considering the gravity of the questions she first laughs. As she begins to respond while shaking her head from left to right as any great thinker would do, letting the download move from the left hemisphere to the right and back, logic to creativity, creativity to logic, she rifts and flows, as examples of what it *could* be start to escape her. She becomes more animated in her body as the metaphysics of spirit, mind and body become engaged with each other, and then it happens: her face tightens and her brows furrow, constricted by the impact of what she herself has just discovered. She firmly states "I'll tell you what freedom is to me – no fear".

Pick up your weapon, soldier, and prepare to strike!

Visual Signs

Movement	Likely Meaning	Action
Small rapid taps	Nibblers (crabs, small fish)	Wait; check bait
Solid downward jerk	Aggressive bite (bass, mackerel)	Prepare to strike
Sustained bend	Fish hooked itself	Start reeling immediately
Slack line tension	Fish swimming toward shore	Reel fast to regain tension

IT'S CALLED FISHING, NOT CATCHING

"Give tanks ..."

SPEECH DEBELLE, AGE 39

Photography taken by Ty Faruki 2022

Striking

There's something like an unfolding happening from here onward, like the third and final act of the movie. This is the part where we start to see the true driving force of the protagonist and why the villain and the hero are not so different. From this point of the journey, the entire thing starts making sense. I bought this gear, I researched this spot, I stuck it out waiting for the bite. I did it for a reason. Maybe what's on the other end of this line is the activation of a new chapter in the story you struggled to claim as your own, especially when relying on old scripts and data you'd convinced yourself were firm truths, when they don't feel so accurate now. The characters couldn't quite develop. This is where the story of what you've been fishing for can start to reveal itself.

The bite indication has shown you a nibble, a knock or a pull and the question is always: is now a good time to strike? Striking too early means the fish doesn't have time to take the bait into its mouth properly. Too late, and often if the fish is small enough, it's taken your bait and gone to hunt new pastures. Something I've had to learn is patience before striking. The excitement propels me into action at the mere sight of knock. Sounds escape of the "woiii" or "oiii" type. But this enthusiasm has meant I've spent a lot of my early days reeling in my line with nothing on it. To stop yourself making the same mistake, consider the fish finding this random bit of lunch and maybe, first, questioning what it is and maybe even why it's there. Attracted by the scent, it may attempt to take a small bite by sucking the bait into its mouth, letting it fall out as it questions the validity of this random feast and only then decide whether it's having it or not. That whole process is what is happening on your rod tip.

Take a moment to wait and observe, and if you're sure that moment of hesitation in the fish is over, and it has indeed taken the bait and hook completely into its mouth, collect your rod and posture and prepare to strike.

What Is Striking?

A strike is the pulling action you make to embed the hook into the fish's mouth. You need to ensure the fish has (at least for the moment) been hooked, preferably in its mouth, meaning you cause less damage to the fish if you need to return it. A fish may pick up your bait and decide to spit it out, even when in motion, once it feels the hook. So, when you do decide to strike, be swift and strike with force.

Striking Timing

To enact a great strike, we need to first go back and think about the bite indication we looked at in the last chapter (*see* page 119). The rod is sitting on its stand, and you see a nibble or knock (a pull is less questionable). If you're sitting, as most beach casters are likely doing at this point – perhaps eating lunch, food not yet fully chewed – and you notice the movement in your peripheral, get up and get next to your rod, close enough to see the bite and pick it up quickly when ready. The angling term used is "letting the bite develop". You want to give the fish a chance not just to investigate but to take the bait and the hook. If you see another nibble or knock, then pick up your rod at this point so you can feel the sensation of the bite in your hands.

On many occasions, I've seen the bite, picked up the rod, focused into my senses, kept still and poised ... and nothing happens. In those instances, I put the rod back down and restart the process of making sure the tension is on the line if needed and go back to watching and waiting but staying close, as there's a good chance another set of bites are imminent.

Now if you pick up the rod, and you *do* feel the sensation and see the tip knocking to match, or, if the rod was leaning over being pulled, then quickly tighten your drag (if you loosened it) and strike. The hook and bait is in the fish's mouth, and this is your opportunity.

Striking Technique

Think about the whole set up. You may have a flapper rig with your hook and bait, and gripper weight on the seabed. The fish has taken the bait into its mouth with a suction motion, which is now pulling the line that connects the weight to the rod. To catch this fish, you will need to pull the weight from the seabed floor as well as hooking the fish.

With one hand on the rod held close to your body for sturdiness and the other on your reel's arm. Pull the rod tip up toward the sky, while simultaneously reeling in the line quickly. This should be done in sync. Without these two movements combined, you'd be reeling in without the force to pull the weight from the seabed and dislodging it quickly enough, or pulling the rod up to dislodge the weight but not retrieving the line, allowing enough slack for the fish to let go.

Fish Behaviour

Now, to explain the behaviour of all the fish around the world would be a book that never ended. But it's also the beauty of fishing. There's a chance to experience something new each time, learn more about this great expanse of the wata and its different forms and the fish in it. The easiest way to categorize them is simply to divide them into big fish and small fish.

The first difference comes with the bite indication. Remember: smaller fish = nibbles/rattles/trembles; larger fish = knocks/pulls. When it's the former, consider a gentler strike, as you may want to keep the fish for live bait or return it for a few different reasons, which we'll look at later in this chapter (*see* page 147). With larger fish, the strike needs to exert more power to stop the fish as it moves away. As you gain more experience, you'll build up a masterful technique for both.

BIG FISH, SMALL FISH

"You never know what's on the end of your line?"

You know those movies that start with a narration that says something like "As far back as I can remember, I always wanted to be a gangster." And by the end of the movie, it has been laid out for us why having such an unhealed dream leads us down a path of wanting and needing something, without knowing what the driving force is. And being a gangster was just the closest reference available to grasp. Needing to be the best at something as opposed to being content with what you are, where you are. As though becoming the best at anything will heal the parts that never heard you were good enough. They call the expression of this the driving force, the ego. Perfect in its design with all credit due, just misaligned mostly and judged for its one purpose and function - feeling safe.

See me, I wanted to be singer, then a rapper, then a paramedic, then a liberation fighter, then back to a rapper. Which is where I have sat comfortably for most of my life. I still *am* a rapper, something my creativity will always take the form of, but I'm not a "big fish" in the game, as I once was, or desire to be anymore. I'm a much smaller fish, with a much bigger perspective now. But being the big fish is what I wanted to be early on in life. That day on the back of the bus, when my audience roared like a stadium, which could have been more akin to Charlie leaving the Big Brother house in one of the show's fake evictions when there weren't more than some sporadic claps, but *no one* could tell Charlie the people did not scream in excitement like at a Michael Jackson concert. Regardless, I felt my future was going to be *big* from that day on. I was sold. I wanted to stretch each of my arms far enough to reach both walls in my bedroom and push outward. I didn't want to be small when I was small. How can I, the one who has had these bruises to the soul, not be here for something greater? Trauma can make you rather self-obsessed, I can say now unashamedly. If being small was some kind of failure on my part that allowed others to harm me, then being big in whatever way I can be will solve this, no?

I signed my record deal in 2007. Made the album *Speech Therapy* in December 2008. Did my first live performance in February 2009.

Quit my day job as a market researcher in May 2009, the day before the album was officially released, which then got nominated for a Mercury Music Prize in July 2009, and won the award for British Album of the Year in September 2009. I then toured for nearly two years straight. Did all the interviews one human could humanly do. Went to the industry events and rubbed shoulders with the biggest celebrities in the world because I, too, was a big fish in the game. An absolute whirlwind of status and celebrity. But man was I broke. Broken, yes, as in fractured on a soul level from trying to hold the pieces together as they swayed like Jenga on the edge of collapse most days. But I also mean financially on my knees. I was a big fish eating at the best restaurants in the world and being handed gift after gift, while being heralded as a new voice, an important voice, a voice deserving of accolades. To the world I would have looked big, but like most new artists with a fresh deal and the world's eyes on them, I was struggling financially. One thing can present as the other. You can hook a fish and swear blind you got yourself a shark, reel it in and this little tiddler appears from the depths to show you size is not the only measure of strength. Things are not ultimately true just because they present so.

That record deal I signed in my naivety meant the album I released would be owned by that label in perpetuity. That means long after I'm gone. One big impactful album that I did not own the rights to. The technical term for ownership of a recording is the master recording copyright or "the masters". A collection of stems (the individual audio files like the drums, or guitar) that make up a whole song. I think about me, a Black woman of Jamaican descent, whose music is owned by a couple of white English men. They're men you never see, just names on contracts who look like small fish on the Tube each morning, heading to the office, seemingly humble and unassuming and nice. While I'm the "star", looking big, loud and not nice. The music industry taught me to be careful of what you wish for. Desiring to be the biggest fish in the sea, just to feel seen, will blind you to who is trying to hook you!

Now with fishing, small fish will catch your big fish. You can catch a small fish and quickly switch to a larger hooked rig, cast it out and wait for something larger to feed on it, thus hooking itself. That smaller fish acts like some kind of ruse. It may be small in its make up but it offers bigger opportunities. Fishing is about thinking about the end goal and how you get there. Steps to success. I've considered many times that with fishing, *I* get to choose. I get to be the one in control. The master of *this* hook and line. The question that haunts me is: What does being the one who does the catching in this practise, instead of the one being caught, give me?

I still don't own my masters for the album. But the stems that once lived on a portable hard drive caught fire about two years after its release, around the same time I discovered what the word "perpetuity" meant. So now, no one has them. It's a huge act of natural destruction to wash away what once was considered a rock-solid agreement. But I still had words and music and creativity. So, I made more stems and more songs, and learned new ways of using my voice.

Sometimes you hook a fish and before it reaches land it shakes itself free. Not everything we catch we're meant to hold on to. But the relationship between what we call a big fish and a small fish is the recognition that neither is more important than the other. They are in fact equal and a reflection of this same reality we're experiencing.

I don't remember the first fish I caught but I *do* remember the first time I fished, and I *do* remember the lessons taught to me through the years of the practise representing the spiritual metanoia I was experiencing. Turning up to fish and having to be more still than I was prepared for, which helped nudge me closer to discovering *why* I wanted to be a big fish and *what* was driving me. Now I'm happy with any catch, no matter the size, because what drives me is different. As you fish more, take note of your own motivations. What does it provide that your soul, or body or mind needed? Drawing attention to the places you deserve to be tended to.

Fish on!

There's nothing more exciting than shouting into the ether "Fish on!" I've been on boats in the deep sea where I'm swaying in the current trying to keep my head up to the horizon to stabilize whatever parts of my brain and bones are rattling me to the point of nausea. But then that bite happens, that strike is right, and I could just as well be back on land.

You've arrived for something, and you intend to find out what that something is.

When you have struck into the bite, you'll feel sensations to let you know a fish is on (hooked), like vibrations or a succession of pulls on the line. With species like stingray that have a wider surface area, it will feel like a solid weight that shall not be moved. As you retrieve the fish toward you it is likely moving through the column and toward the shoreline, but stronger fish will move left or right in fight instead. If this happens, hold the line steady without reeling in. There is no need to fight too much and cause more tension on the line than there already is with you both pulling in opposite directions. Give it a moment until the fish is calmer, check what's around you and start the retrieving process when you feel less resistance.

Lure Fishing Bites

As you're already holding the rod, the bite indication will be felt and responded to immediately. The retrieve of your lure combined with the bite of the fish means the fish is hooked instantly. Just keep retrieving steadily when you feel that bite.

Deep Sea Fishing Bites

If you are resting your rod in a holder as when trolling fishing (fishing with the bait trailing behind a boat), then let the bite develop into something that is unmistakable. The wata itself will cause the rod to rise and dip in the swell or the boat you're on could be causing waves as the engine pushes the wata, making the rod bounce. Retrieving this kind of set up, which is heavy, should be done when you are sure. When it's an unmistakable pull down of the rod, position yourself well (maybe even sit down) and strike as you would when coastal fishing Use your body weight and lean back as you pull. If you are drop/ bottom fishing and holding the rod, strike as you would with beach fishing, pulling upward while retrieving.

Tips for a Better Strike

- Stay calm and remind yourself to breathe. The stillness will help you be more in tune with your gear and the elements, so you can feel and see the bite.
- Practising a strike even if unsure about whether it's a bite or not will build muscle memory. So, if you are unsure and worried, you'll miss it, go for it.
- Adapt, adapt, adapt. Adjust your drag to see if it changes your striking chances. Try different rigs with different size hooks or different sizes and coloured lures.
- If your drag was loosened for fishing larger fish, then remember, remember, remember to tighten your drag before your strike! If not, you'll strike without enough tension.

Like casting, which is poetry in movement, striking has its place in the overall dance. It's the pull that we've had as humans and have had to do since the beginning – the beginning, as in the start of this experience and life we know now. In Zanzibar, the fisherman, along with any community members who want to join in the ritual of pulling their fishing nets back in from the sea, get one behind the other in a tug-of-war line, reaching forward and pulling the line that connects the net with hopefully a good number of fish to sell at the market and some to bring home too.

Consider how, as we're born, gravity pulls us from the birth canal or with the help of knowledgeable and gentle hands onto this rock.

To strike is to pull. This is a reminder that we are always pulling energy, people and experiences to us, and pulling ourselves away. With the art of fishing, the rarity it brings is the uncertainty of what we're striking and pulling, along with the comfort and excitement in the not knowing.

Reeling In

The strike was right. The fish is on. The rod is in your hand and you can feel the rattle of the rod as the line is being pulled back into the sea, left to right, up to the surface and back down into the wata column. Here's where it gets real. It's the part in our monthly hook ups where people who have never fished or are new to fishing start to get the dread. I get it. Where there is excitement for what could be, there is also fear. You know when you're swimming at the beach, and the most nervous of the crew has to say something like "Guys, what just touched my foot?" just to remind us all of the film we watched and never forgot. We're both horrified and humoured in chorus. That is the dread that envelopes the newbies and experienced anglers alike because – heavens, what if it's a stingray? Which it could be on any day. What if it's a shark? Even in the UK, it could be. What if it's just a fish and I'm pulling this thing in to inevitably be here on land with me, a place I just about feel at home half the time. Me looking at him and him looking at me, and we're looking at each other both knowing it's on me to do the thing that comes next. But don't worry, we'll look at what to do when you've landed the fish. Once you get your breath back!

What Is Reeling In?

To reel in is to retrieve your line, which we covered in the last chapter (*see* pages 104, 109 and 121), but now with a fish hooked and attached to it. We want to do this with as much control as possible to ensure safety.

Let's break this down into the three components that work in unison for this process to happen:

The Rod

- *You want to keep your rod tip facing upward to allow it to bend in the way it is designed to. This flex absorbs the shocks and keeps the tension in your line. Try and keep it at a 45–60° angle as you reel in, so the fish's head is facing upward.*
- *For larger fish you'll want to use the pump and reel action. Once you feel some strength to the fish by its weight or pull, rather than just reeling in with your rod angled up as before, lift the rod up higher like when striking to pull the fish toward you. Then lower the rod back down and reel in simultaneously. Lift and pull again, lower and reel in. This will take a little longer, but it ensures you don't snap your line as you both pull in opposite directions.*

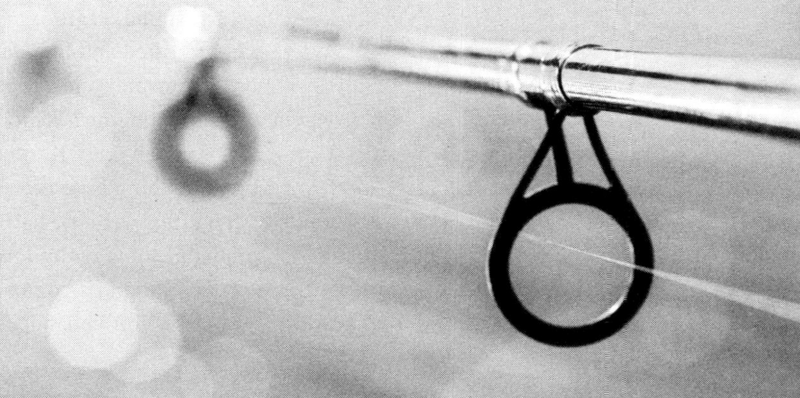

The Reel

- *With any size fish, you must be reeling in to bring the fish in or up from below, if on a boat. If the fish isn't large, then give a rhythmic and constant reel. You don't need to rush this process even if it is small and the urge is to crank up that thing. A steady retrieve keeps the fish safe.*
- *If it's a big fish and you go to reel but nothing happens as the strength of the fish resists, loosen the drag a little to lessen the strain on the line. You can tighten again once you feel in a better position to do so.*

The Body

- Plant your feet and ground yourself. Look down and around so you know where you can move if you need to. If you're on a boat and it's swaying in the current, then widen your stance like those who have mastered not holding onto the rail on the London Underground as the carriage rocks –they sway their centre of gravity just enough to redress the balance.
- Consider how your body feels. It's easy to forget that you may be in an awkward position, half-sitting, half-standing, and the adrenaline has made you check out of your own edges. Be kind to your body.

Reading the Pull

Now you can never be sure of what fish you have until it breaks the swell or the colour starts to appear from the deep blue. But while reeling it in, combined with your data (is there a shoal of something or a particular fish breeding in this area?) you can get a sense of what it *might* be. You may have chosen your lure specifically for this area on a recommendation. Or maybe you used flattie rigs and got the tremble-like bite, indicating it's exactly the species you intended to catch. Many anglers can tell you with a great chance of being correct what fish they have, just from the bite and the vibrations as they're reeling it in.

Pulling Small Fish

- Mackerel, like most smaller fish, are known to shake more. The energy is erratic in the same way they feed, quickly changing direction as you reel in. Mackerel season is a favourite of mine. Not only is fresh mackerel the king of flavour for me, but the fight is fun. They're also a great catch for children learning to fish and a super sustainable food source.
- Just keep reeling in. Smaller fish can shake so much they can shake loose from the hook. They're also more prone to damage, so like the gentler strike, the pull should be controlled and measured as you steadily reel them in.

Pulling Big Fish

- Fish like pollock, jack or pompano are more likely to make a run when they realize they are hooked. On a boat the rod tip will pull down with some real force as the fish attempts to swim back down to the deep after swimming up to launch at its prey. You'll feel that strong pull once, twice, three times. Steady yourself and hold tight. At the shore, they may attempt to swim in the opposite direction and pull the line from your reel. Loosen your drag a bit and let it run, then tighten again. The aim of the game with larger fish is to let them get tired first. Then in the moments of calm, reel in again.
- If they pull down, make sure you have a good grip of the rod. If they swim away and your reel sings as the line is being pulled from it, let it run. You don't want to be pulling or reeling when this happens as, remember, the line can only handle so much force. It may even give you a chance to compose yourself or catch a break. When it stops, go back to the pull up and reel action.

Pulling Deep Sea or Sport Fish

- These are your species like tuna and sailfish, and people spend a *lot* of money travelling to the most famous reefs in the world to get a chance at catching them. You'll 100 per cent be on a boat for this offshore fishing. The rods will be set up already, so you can sit and use your body as weight and to pump back and forth while reeling in.

Working with the Elements

Current and Waves

- Work with the wata, not against it. If you're lure fishing and reeling something in, but you need to get it up onto a rock you're standing on, let the wave help lift the fish so you're not yanking it up with your rod. You can do the same with shore fishing by letting the wave bring the fish in. If you see a big wave about to break then take a couple of steps backward at the same time, so you have less work on your arms.

Obstacles

- If you're fishing near underwater rocks or a pier, the fish is likely to head to those for cover. This means your line could get wrapped, making it nearly impossible to get the fish and your gear back. Physically move to the left or right if you need to. You can lift your rod tip if the fish isn't too heavy to move it around objects or through weeds or kelp.

Slack Line

If you are reeling in and it suddenly feels like the fish has disappeared, it could be swimming toward you, so keep reeling. As you do so, the weight and shake of the fish will reappear as you reel in enough of the slack to catch up with it. Because of this slack, it's easy to question whether anything is hooked, but you're better off reeling in completely with nothing than risking losing your catch by not completing the process.

Landing Your Catch

There will be a moment when your catch appears in the shallows or from the deep and you can see its colours appear but not yet in focus, as though you're entering wakefulness from a sleeping state. When the muscles of your neck pull forward as you try to see what you've caught, along with the other anglers either side of you who are as eager as you are to know, the moment reminds you that the ocean really does hold the stories.

What is Landing?

Landing a fish is the term used to describe how to get it from the wata on to land. My cousin used to have a pitbull terrier that he would let me walk when I was a pre-teen. Now when I say let me walk, I mean let me hold the lead while the dog walked me. I remember once, my cousin (purposely, no doubt) made a sudden dash across the park without warning and this gentle giant of a beast nearly yanked my soul out of my right arm. This was hilarious to my cousin, as I gurgled sounds that made no sense but would have meant "Help!" if they could. As my two human feet tried to keep up with this pitbull's four, mine buckled and gave way as I hit the grass, rolled, and came to a stop star shape on the ground.

Why am I sharing this? I'm drawing the parallel with what it means to land a fish. You are holding the other end of the line, and this species designed to move, change direction instantly and travel huge distances is pulling in another direction. The fish may be small, so the landing could be little or no hassle and a matter of just reeling in. But it could be a larger species, which means you must move and respond to it. Either way, the aim is to stay grounded, consider what's around you and the fish – and stand firm!

Landing Techniques

- Move closer to the shore because your fish is getting closer as well, especially if it's small. Small fish don't hold up well to bangs or scrapes, so landing them right at the shore means you can easily return them if you're not keeping them instead of pulling along rocks or shingle.
- For a large fish, walk backward a few steps as it breaks the shoreline. Fish can at this point shake their head in panic and release themselves as the feel the exit from the wata. Keep the tension on the line.

Landing on a Pier or Rocks

You don't want to winch the fish onto rocks a lot higher than the surface, or up a pier if you can help it. In doing this you could snap your rod, which isn't designed to be a forklift. Or you could snap the line releasing your gear and the hooked fish from the weight of the gravity. It could also be dangerous if you're trying to hang over a side of the pier or lean over the side of the rocks. There is no fish in the world worth falling for. If someone has a long net, which is common on piers, ask if they can help you land your fish. They'll likely already be on it and on their way as they watch you reel it in. If no one is around and you don't have a net to scoop up the fish, then look for anything nearby that you can use as a landing point, like steps.

Tips for Landin

- *Regardless of which type of fishing you'r doing, as they approach the edge, fish wi likely make a last-ditch attempt to resist. you've reeled your fish in closer, lift your rod even more to keep the fish's head fac upward. This will control its shake.*

- *When fishing for mackerel and using five so feathers on one rig, you could be brin in five fish. But with this many fish at onc you need to walk backward, even if you'r a rock or a pier (but only if there's the sp of course) as there will be a lot of flappi about going on at once. The aim is to ge fish onto land, as soon as you can, to giv yourself more room to work.*

- *Be prepared. When setting up your gear the day, think ahead to how you're going land your fish. Will you need a bucket or net, perhaps to keep it as live bait or to l it recover in some wata for a few minute before returning it?*

To Hold or to Net?

When coastal fishing, you'll need to use your hands to pick up the fish, or gloves or even a dish towel if you don't want that direct contact. But if pulling the fish up from the side of a boat, kayak, pier or up some rocks, you're better off netting the fish. Here's a closer look at the two options.

Hand Landing

It's a good idea to have a bucket of seawater during your sessions. You can use this to clean your hands throughout and also wet them before handling the fish. Dry hands can strip the protective layer from the fish's scales and leave it prone to infection, especially if you use oils on your skin. You can also keep the fish in this wata to help it recover before returning it if the process of retrieving took some time, or for bleeding the fish once dispatched, which we'll talk more about shortly (*see* page 147).

To hold the fish, the best place is behind the gills with one hand and at the beginning of its tail with the other. For fish with a more visible and larger gill plate, slide your index and second finger under the gill cover while trying your best not to touch the gills. Hold it firmly as it may shake and fall. For larger fish with softer bellies like a Smooth-hound (a shark species), support the belly with your other hand to protect its organs from stretching. For flat fish, hold the entire body in the palm of your hand. Try not dangle a fish by their tail as this could damage the spine.

Some fish have sharp fins so be careful with these species and take time to consider your hand placement rather than grabbing at it. Use what's around you. If you have a cool box, place the fish on it to help settle it and free up at least one hand to allow you to move to the next stage of unhooking the fish.

Net Landing

When you've reeled in until you are at your leader line and you can see the fish, lower your net so it is either, under the fish or just behind it. If you approach with the net from the front, the fish will naturally attempt to swim away from it. You don't want to chase the fish with the net, but instead try to steer the fish onto and over the net with your rod.

Once the fish is over the net you can lift it to land. When the fish is on the boat or landed wherever you are, choose the safest place to lay it down so you can quickly move on to unhooking.

Here's the thing, you will over time forget your first cast. Not because it's not important, but because you are practising the motion, the dance, and that gets lost in the process, in the best way. But you will likely remember your first catch. You will probably have pictures to show it. Give yourself a round of applause. Pat yourself on the back. Make an audible celebration of your achievement. Put your two fingers in the air for yourself. You are now fishing *and* catching.

Once you're back at your base, you can identify the fish species and measure it. This is a good time to decide quickly, if you would like to keep the fish or return it. Either way, the hook needs to be removed from the fish now.

Removing the Hook

You've got to learn to unhook – the careful process of separating fish from the line. Your steadiness is the protection you will offer the fish. It's perhaps the point when you get to become your most delicate. It's rather intimate. You hold in your hands something that lives, just like you. Something that has fed us as part of the natural ecosystem for millennia. This act is one of gratitude and care.

All this time spent buying the gear, and the days with no catch because you brought lugworm and the fish wanted crab. But you finally found a rhythm and it all started coming together. Perhaps it was just after a storm, so the fish were closer to the shore and the wind was south-easterly or south-south-easterly. The bait had been uprooted from the storm, so the fish were already on a feeding frenzy when you arrived. Or maybe it was simply because today was your day.

As obvious as it sounds, that special time will not set up a scheduled Zoom meeting with you, but it absolutely *will* arrive. In between screams of accomplishment and slight terror, my advice in this moment is to take a breath and regulate yourself.

Last week a young man who was fishing a short way down the beach from me started heading my way. He was too far away for me to be sure he was walking toward *me*, so I glanced over then looked back at my rod, ears up like a dog who hears the word "outside". That crunch sound of boots on beach stones got closer, so naturally I looked again, London awareness kicking in asking, *Who is this? And what do they want with me?* In fairness, it's kept me safe. Men have been dangerous, even though I'm dangerous too. As he got close enough, I asked, "You alright?" in my deepest chest voice with an upward tilt of my head, face looking straight at him and eyes slightly squinting. He replied, "Hey, I've just caught a fish, but I can't get the hook out. Can you help?" I know exactly how that feels.

Unhooking Techniques

1. Tools

- Have your pliers at the ready when you set up your gear, so maybe on the cooler already or within easy reach.
- A disgorger may be needed if the hook is in deep.
- Think about where you can lay the fish down to free up at least one hand for the unhooking process like a cooler box.

2. Pos-i-tion

- If the fish is still hooked and attached to your line, you may have to give yourself some slack by opening the reel arm or loosening the drag and pulling out some line. Do this so the rod can be placed back on the stand or rested on the floor, out of your way.
- Think about your body. These knees of mine don't work like they used to. So rather than crouch, I like to rest on both knees on a jacket or a tea towel. Or just pull up my chair.
- If confident enough, you can remove the hook with one hand while holding the fish with the other.

3. Precision

- If the hook is through the fish's mouth or lips, use the pliers to grip the shank and pull the hook backward. This means in the opposite direction to its entry point.
- Fish teeth range from virtually non-existent tiny teeth to human-looking teeth and some are extremely sharp fangs. Take a moment to look at what they're working with, don't just jump in there. This is akin to you in a dentist's chair, laid back, the light shining down on you with someone you can't quite make out because of their protective clothing, heading your way with tools.
- Examine the hook position and imagine, even act out, the backward pull first, before attempting it.

Hook Damage

I can often take my eyes off the rod to set up a new rig or try and find my lighter in every pocket, and when I look back at the rod, it is bouncing – fish on! Because the fish has had more time without striking and being mouth-hooked, it can swallow the hook completely. When I've reeled in this fish and see that hook is just too deep to remove without causing the fish damage, I prefer to dispatch the fish and then remove the hook after. I use the fillets as bait for that same session or store it away for another day. Or I fillet the fish at home and pack it into sea salt, which gives me saltfish in a few weeks, for Caribbean-style fritters. Returning a damaged fish to the sea means its life may be short and difficult.

Foul Hook

Sometimes you can reel in a fish and it's what's called "foul hooked". This means that instead of being hooked in the mouth, it could have been caught in the belly, tail or fin. It generally happens when a fish grabs at your bait or lure but misses and, as you strike, it gets hooked elsewhere on its body. If this happens and you want to release the fish, unhook it as you would with the tools (*see* page 145), but be sure to allow more time for it to recover. You can do this by placing it in a bucket or cooler with just sea wata or holding the fish around its belly in the shoreline allowing the wata to pass through its gills for some time. If it's a large wound or around its organs, again, dispatching it may be the better choice.

Dispatching or Releasing

You can fish for the sport and recreation of it. Catching a lot of the same species on the same or concurrent sessions? *Argh, not again for dinner! I'll leave it.* Or, if you get the fish you've always wanted to catch but know it's not one you'll enjoy eating, you may choose to return it. Whether you have the privilege to choose, or not, this fish is here now, in your hands. Regardless of what you do, honour its life and the moment you've shared. Say thank you if it feels right.

Decide if you want to catch (keep and dispatch) the fish or release it.

Here are the tools that will help you.

- Regulation measuring tool so you adhere to size regulations if keeping the fish.
- Club or rock for larger species with stronger protective layers like dogfish or barracuda.
- Knife for dispatching and bleeding.

Dispatching a Fish

1. Be decisive and quick. Hesitation usually makes things worse. Use a knife or a sharp object (the sharper the better) to cut through the top of the fish's head, immobilizing it and ending its life swiftly. You can also use the technique of pulling its head backward toward its body quickly, and instantly immobilizing it. For fish with stronger scales and skin, you can use a club or rock forcefully on the top of its head, knocking it unconscious.

2. If you plan to eat the fish, you may want to bleed it by cutting the gills next. This process allows the blood to be released out of its veins, rather than into its flesh, so maintaining freshness

and colour. I prefer to gut the fish in the sea or the body of wata rather than at home. This maintains absolute freshness, uses the wata to clean it and the tools, as well as providing an additional food source for other fish with the parts we do not consume going back.

3. You can now leave the fish in a cooler or on ice, especially in warmer weather or on a boat. If you don't have anywhere to store the fish while you continue fishing, I've seen people dig a hole in the sand or shingles and bury the fish, as under the surface retains a cool temperature while protecting the fish from the heat of the sun.

4. Practise using selective harvesting. Keep only what you intend to eat, unless a fish is too damaged to return. Follow what the sea is offering currently. If you keep catching one type of fish, the ocean is saying it is on offer. There is a fine balance, and the Earth knows better than we do. Check your local size limitations. There may be a species that is under threat, so protect it if you can. There are also invasive species that you are advised to always keep, like lionfish in the Caribbean. Always check the species of fish you catch. Lionfish are depleting the populations of everything else around them, but their spikes are venomous and will cause a lot of pain if they prick you. In the UK the Greater Weever fish also has venomous fins that cause pain.

Returning the Fish

1. Assess the fish's condition to ensure it is strong enough to swim away. Can you see signs of injuries? If it has fins on the top of its body, those will be standing up to attention if it's strong and ready to swim away. If not, or it's not moving much, it may be spent and need more time to recover in a bucket of seawater or by you holding it along its belly in the shoreline until it's ready to swim off unaided.

2. Watch the fish as it swims away. It can get confused in the swell after being on this strange thing called land, then accidently swim back to shore. You may need to direct it with a soft nudge. Also,

consider where you release it, so avoid doing so near your engine if on a boat, or from a great height onto anything other than deep enough wata.

Conservation and Responsibility

Each decision you make impacts the ecosystem, but don't expect that impact to only be shown to you by these colonial laws. You also need to listen to your innate connection. Release an under-sized fish, not just because you've been told to, but because you can wait for the next catch and give this one more time to grow and repopulate the species. Listen to the locals, the long-time anglers, the people in the village and the community. Hear their stories. They can be vastly different from what's in the news.

A Deeper Meaning?

The first description of the word "dispatch" in the Oxford Dictionary that came up when I did an online search is:

> verb
> gerund or present participle: **dispatching**
> 1. send off to a destination or for a purpose.

How interesting! In angling terms, we say "release" to return it back to the wata alive, and "dispatch" as the term to end its journey there, killing it as humanely as possible. But by the Oxford definition, either way, we're sending it off.

As for ourselves, we must also assess the hook placement and any damage from scrapes and bumps, giving ourselves a good look over in the mirror. See the light and shadow parts. Your hook marks may still be there, like a fashion choice in your early twenties, healed over but still slightly visible.

Consider that to unhook, it takes a force. It takes precision. You must go back the way you got here. Any other direction will create a deeper, wider, wound. Like a knot, you must take steps back. A regression.

The hook is a tool, to get, grab, secure, tether, hold, but it's not meant to stay. The hook is *not* meant to stay. To keep or to release are both to dispatch some part of a journey.

Food Sovereignty

Once you've decided to keep your catch and dispatched it, this next step is important for maintaining its freshness. Many of us are used to buying fish from the supermarket. Being from a dense inner city, it's what I was accustomed to. How the fish is caught, dispatched, and cared for, is the difference between food that is at its optimum freshness and best for our bodies, or farmed, produced and packaged to travel for huge distances before it arrives to us filled with chemicals for large scale consumerism.

Good Friday has always been a day in a Caribbean home when fish is brought home double-wrapped in two plastic bags. One is to hold the fish, the other to hold any juices that may run out on your way home. Family and friends meet at the designated house of whoever is managing the big cook up. The origins of this tradition of eating fish on Good Friday are a mixture of two events in the Christian faith: the day Jesus was able to feed five thousand people with just five loaves of bread and two fish with the power of God, and Good Friday, which commemorates the Crucifixion. Or something like that. It was always the food that was the highlight for me, not the religion I'm afraid.

On Good Friday fish is fried and topped with an escovitch mix of scotch bonnet peppers, carrots and onions cooked in vinegar, a little sugar and spices like pimento seeds. It's served with sliced hard dough bread and slathered in butter. It's truly a divine combination. Now this is not the only dish served, but it is the heart and soul of the event.

When buying the fish at the market for Good Friday, most people ask the fishmongers to gut and clean it, so the bulk of the work is done before you get home. But because of the distance that fish may have travelled, it's nearly impossible to guarantee their freshness or the conditions they've been kept in while travelling. Because of this, it's common to need to clean the fish with vinegar and/or lime once you get home. Eyes and heads will roll if your guests are not assured that your fish has been cleaned and prepped this way. When the fish are coming from the market in this densely populated place, it's no surprise that we need to become the cleaning police.

Here's the difference though. When you start catching fish yourself, you'll notice the difference straight away in their quality and hygiene. The eyes are brightly coloured, not with a kind of film over the top that develops over time once dispatched. Fresh fish smells of the sea, not fishy at all. The flesh is firm, not softened in the process of being frozen and thawed again. There really is nothing more delicious than freshly caught fish, and it asks for way less bringing back to cleanliness or life.

The traditions we have as diasporic people are held onto tightly and so they should be. What at first seems to be layers of culture, can actually be a practical response to the conditions. The cleaning or seasoning police is a phrase used on social media. But aren't they just people doing their best to keep a tradition of good health with food that is not in a good state when purchased? Lime not only tenderises meat but cleans it and adds flavour. I love the quote by Resma Menakem, from their book *My Grandmother's Hands*: "Trauma decontextualized in a person looks like personality. Trauma decontextualized in a family looks like family traits. Trauma decontextualized in a people looks like culture."

Now that you have caught fish, we should talk about what to do with it to keep it fresh and prepare it for a delicious meal, however your heart whispers to.

Bleeding the Fish

This is a great idea if you plan to fillet your fish. Bleeding allows the blood to run from the gills after it's dispatched, instead of into the flesh, keeping the fillet free from blood lines.

Hold the fish firmly and use scissors or a knife to cut the gills on both sides. If you have a bucket of sea wata, place the fish back in to act as a rinse aid, or use the wata you have around you to rinse it off. You can also place the fish back into your cool box to bleed for a while, but you may wish to rinse the cooler out after a few minutes.

Filleting the Fish

1. Position the fish well on a flat surface. If you're right-handed, the fish's head should be on your right, and if left-handed, the fish's head should be on your left.

2. Make the first cut behind the gill plate. Use your fingers or knife to check where this plate begins and ends. You're going to slice along the gill plate, moving into the flesh until you hit the spine. This can be done in one slicing movement.

3. Now with the tip of your knife, start right behind the fish's head, starting from the gill plate, cut, and gently run it down the length of the body until you reach the tail. Then from the top again, using the tip, cut again all the way down further into the cut you already made. Go further in each time, with just the tip of the knife. Even if it seems tedious to start with, you are making more of an incision each time rather than a deep cut at once.

4. By the second or third time, you should feel the bones on the tip of your knife and may even hear them. This is what you want. As you make your way down, you'll begin separating the fillet from the bone.

5. Keep repeating the process, keeping you blade angled down and in contact with the bones until you reach the spine, in between the sides of both fillets. Then angle your blade up to essentially cut over the bone.

6. Once past it, you are at the second half of this fillet. Angle your knife back down again towards the bones and use the same technique to completely remove the fillet from one side of the fish.

7. Flip the fish over and repeat the process.

Removing the Skin

If you're planning on having the fillet deep-fried in batter or flour and you also want to remove the skin, first place the fillet, skin-side down, on your chopping board. Make an initial small cut into the flesh but without going through the skin entirely, about an inch (2.5cm) from top of the fillet. Then hold that small piece of the fillet at the top firmly with one hand, which becomes your anchor point.

Angle the knife downward toward the skin and run it along where the flesh and skin meet, in the opposite direction to your hand. You can use a kind of shimmy technique to work the knife along the fillet, while also gently pulling the small bit you are holding, until the flesh is completely separated from the skin.

Tip: Don't throw away the rest of the fish away – the head, especially of a larger fish, still has a lot of meat, as does the backbone, and these parts can be used to make a delicious soup or stock. All of the leftover fish parts like the guts can be used as fertiliser in your garden. If you're filleting at the wata's edge, throw what you don't want back to the ocean to feed other fish.

Cleaning the Whole Fish

If you want to cook the fish whole, you'll need to clean and gut it.

1. If at home, a great trick for scaling your fish (removing the scales) is to first clean and fill your sink or large bowl with wata. Hold the fish under it with one hand and using a knife, rub the scales of the fish from the tail to the head. Doing this underwater stops the scales from flying around your kitchen.

2. Now gut the fish by placing it on a flat surface and inserting the knife into the small hole near the middle of the fish. Cut upward until you have reached the pectoral fin. You don't need to cut too deeply. To cut this fin takes a little more force or even scissors, but you do want to cut right through it completely, so you can completely open the fish past the gills.

3. You'll then, using your hands, be able to pull the gills out and down forcefully, which in turn also pulls out the guts that are connected in one go.

4. Once the fins and organs are removed, run under a tap and use your hands to clean the empty captivity. You can use the top of the knife to cut open the skin closet to the bones so you can properly clean the blood tract.

5. Pat the fish to dry and season and cook as desired.

Sustainable Catching

It can be easy to see the fish as just the fillet, which is common in British culture. But there has been a rise in chefs using knowledge from indigenous cultures, as well as reaching further back into older British cultures, to better use what they have and create less waste. It's not just about waste though. Flavour is a big reason to keep more than the fillet. Any meat on anything will have the most flavour when closest to the bones. So, a bone-in sirloin steak will have a richer flavour than the fillet. Additionally, "offcuts" can have a rich flavour as well as a greater amount of nutritional value.

The head and collars of fish are amazing grilled as well. The collar specifically carries a lot of meat that isn't removed as part of the filleting process, as half of it is above the gill plate. Try using a large knife (if you feel safe to do so) or scissors and cut the head in what's called a butterfly. This means cutting until it can open, but not all the way through. Season and grill it and, once cooked, add a good amount of lemon juice to balance the oily rich flavour.

The offal of fish are similar to those of other animals. This means the liver, kidneys and heart (preferably on a larger fish, to make it worthwhile) can be eaten as well. Livers and the fishes roe are probably best pan-fried, after being coated and dusted in a little seasoned flour, as they become delicate when cooked. The roe of fish like salmon are often added to sushi or as a garnish on seafood dishes.

Try different styles of cooking: open fire or BBQ, oven or pan roasting or smoking. The more you experiment, the more cultures will open to you with more flavours from around the world.

As I have mentioned, I prefer to clean and prepare the fish I catch right there at the shoreline before I even bring it home. This is something my gran told me she used to do, in one of our long talks as she edged closer to being physically further away. This is when her hands, which I watched make just about everything as a child and that without question could have tied a Dropper Loop Knot in her sleep, were becoming tight and restricted in their movement. So, she would look down at them, like foreign things, and make a fist to encourage them to remember what they were capable of.

She told me (and retold many times) the story of how she came from the countryside of Mandeville in Jamaica, where she and her family were born and raised. She would make the all-day trip to the coastline for freshly caught fish whenever a celebration, such as Good Friday, was at hand. Or when she needed to give her husband space to "cool down likkle bit". Fish was for special occasions.

She would ask the fisherman to gut the fish, which he'd oblige and even offer the service for free if she asked the right man, on the right day. Or she would gut them herself right there at the beach with whoever had travelled up with her that day. Either way, she would enjoy some fish cooked up right on the wata's edge for lunch. She said she'd dip the fish freshly cooked on the coals into the sea to add salt. This was essentially a day trip to collect fish, so she didn't take along seasonings or – as this was back in the 1940s – a portable BBQ. That meant the sea and the freshness of the catch were the seasoning, along with the taste of smoke from the fire for the umami.

What my gran and others of that generation engaged in, is what we are engaging in now, when we catch and cook. It's a form of sovereignty. She herself, the fishermen who caught fish that day, the bus that got her to and from the beach, and the food she so loved to exclaim as brain food – healthy and suitable – were all part of a culture that supported the economy and the health of its people.

We are choosing to engage with our food source directly each time we cast out our line, whether we keep our catch that day or not. The systems may have created borders, but the only true border we humans have is the ocean's depth.

What Is Food Sovereignty?

The following quotation from La Via Campesina gives a good summary of what food sovereignty is.

> *The term "food sovereignty" was first coined in 1996 by the international peasant movement La Via Campesina at the World Food Summit. It emerged as a concept to emphasize the right of peoples and nations to control their own food systems, placing producers and democracy at the center of food systems.*
>
> *Food sovereignty is the right of people to healthy and culturally appropriate food produced through ecologically sound and sustainable methods and their right to define their own food and agriculture systems* (La Via Campesina, 2022).*

Colonial borders now control the oceans and this controls who is afforded food sovereignty. The marginalization of local farmers and indigenous communities' way of life and livelihood is interrupted by the colonial industrial powers, whose focus is on instant food sources and their constant availability. They don't follow species migration periods, breeding areas or the disruption of the eco-system of all surrounding species.

Food security is a huge issue. Even in the UK, food banks are needed for working class people, who are spending eight hours a day at work

---

* https://www.researchgate.net/figure/Six-pillars-of-food-sovereignty-Food-sovereignty-is-based-on-six-pillars-or-approaches_fig2_355187464

but are unable to afford enough to eat. On the surface food sovereignty is about people being able to eat but it also highlights the rights of communities and people to have control without governmental pressures, over their cultural and social relationship to that food. It's really a form of social justice. Fishing is an opportunity for us to regain some sovereignty over the food we catch and consume.

There's this kind of policing of Black and Brown people that can happen even when fishing with one or two rods from the shore. It's the trickle down of whiteness from the colonial mindset that makes some people the arms and legs of the monster that only eats itself. A random angler, keeping a watchful eye on your cooler and its contents, or reminding you without warrant about the legal size of a cod. There can be a pressure just to take what you will eat today, as they proclaim they do: "This will do for me tea." Alluding to anything more being un-British. But remember food sovereignty and what it means. Are you being some kind of upright member of society by only fishing for yourself that day? Your neighbour, who hasn't been here from their country of origin for a long time, might love some fresh fish. They may be from a place where it was abundant, but without access now, or maybe they don't have the time or space or intel to reclaim this part of their life miss the taste of fresh fish. Wouldn't they love two freshly caught fish too? Food sovereignty is also an act of anti-capitalism and individualism.

How We Can Engage in Wider-scale Food Sovereignty

Participate in Fishing Communities

Are there groups near you like We Are Black Fish where you can learn to fish together and share your catch? Where you're not just learning the skills of catching, but also how to prep and cook food. Not all people have grown up with cooking food like fish as a constant in their lives. If this is you, it's a great way to engage with people who have this skillset.

Think about what skills you can you bring to the community. Can you encourage others in the group to attend? Can you share knowledge in some other way?

Support Local Farmers

Do you have access to buying fish (meat or vegetables) from local farmers and fisheries? Are their co-ops local to you? Are there food banks you can help and items you can contribute that will likely sit in your cupboard?

Grow Your Own Food

Like fishing as a form of food sovereignty, growing your own veg is also part of a lifestyle change. Is there a local garden or allotment you can support or use to grow produce in? You can grow herbs and veg on your windowsill with very little space. It doesn't have to be a big production.

Cook What You Have

My partner and I like to challenge ourselves to every so often cook the food we have instead of buying more constantly. What about that tin of butter beans that's been sitting in the cupboard since I don't know when? Or the pack of noodles that's been there about the same amount of time? Try using the herbs that are wilting, to make a herb butter or boil them to make medicinal teas to help cleanse and warm the body.

Reduce Waste

As when filleting, think about what you'll do with the parts you're not keeping, as well as how you can add them to your catalogue of food and flavours. Start your own compost, which can be used to fertilize soil to further help growing other foods.

Be an Ally

It's important to be an ally for other people's cultures and experiences – without imposing upon them your beliefs or casting judgement. Learning about other cultures' food practices provides knowledge for your own toolkit and means you can be an ally in the places that are not welcome or quite rightly not wanting to be.

As we approach the conclusion of this journey into the art of fishing, we're in a place when we have caught the fish and may even be cooking it up. The journey means that what seems like the obvious reason for fishing, which is considered the catching, doesn't even register until fish on. But like the deeper meaning of dispatching or releasing, this is a life we hold and a way of life that reaches further than this moment. Food sovereignty is an invitation to reclaim what we eat and how it is sourced. It's a natural progression from reclaiming the coastline itself. We're engaging with an ancient food source and positively disrupting the industrial food systems.

Did You Blank Yet?

There's a term in the angling world that can create shame or leave you disheartened. But it simply means I was there today, and I tried. It's called "blanking" and means there was no catch in today's session. When I tell you, I blankety blanked in my early days. I was thinking about the gear and its uses, what gear to pack and not pack, the weather conditions, the hours I had spare to make the session even happen. I was tripping wires in my brain to understand if that was a bite or was it my own foot as I walked past the rod and went from seated to standing like an inspector taking a closer look. I was standing up, willing the rod to show me – *is that you, fish?* I would sit back down, get up again to double check. There are days when it's more complicated than smooth sailing and serene.

Currently it's August and it's been three weeks since I've caught a fish I've wanted to keep. The bites have been few and far between. But it's not just me, hardly anyone is catching. It's important to see what others are saying to recognise that the timings of migrations and seasons can change year to year, and you're not doing anything wrong. The groups are lit up with theories on the slow fishing. Some are saying, it's because the spider crabs (that are invasive) are eating the bait before the fish get a chance. This tracks. I keep getting this slight pull down on the rod tip. When I retrieve the line after waiting for 15 minutes or so to check the bait, the hooks are stripped clean or, sometimes, the line that holds the hook is completely severed. It's certainly giving crab. The suggestion was to add a float to the line just in front of the hook to keep the hook and bait off the seafloor where the crabs hunt. I tried that. Still no bites though.

Others have said it's because the tuna are here in the summer and they're eating up all the fish. Now unless I can breathe underwater and see this happening for myself, sure, I guess. It tracks. "The trawlers! It's the trawlers cleaning everything up!" say the locals. This also tracks. It's been a north-easterly wind for a while. "Wind from the east and the fish bite least," as the saying goes. Hard to say, without the wind changing again to compare. Regardless of why its currently slow, we're all still out there – trying and waiting for the "tide to turn" in our favour again. And it will.

Watch out for what you tell yourself in these times. Be careful of how you speak to and about yourself. Be careful of what stories you are sowing into your make up. It's called fishing, not catching. It's returning home to your carved out piece of peace. That peace may not arrive instantly or in the same quantity each time, but that's control. Fishing is freedom and freedom can't be measured in the same way.

Even the days when you blank, you can feel the weather may not have been perfect for the session. The wind bounced so much you couldn't make out whether it's a bite or not. But the weather was perfect for you. You may have needed a little breeze to cool your body down as it rises those couple of degrees, as your womb matches the moon's cycle. You may have needed a light rain, even if only to remind you that your hair is just hair, when you've been taught it should constantly be managed.

Even the most experienced anglers have days when they blank. I've heard some say they've blanked only because they didn't catch their target species but caught just about everything else. To them, that was a blank.

At the beginning of this book I had one of those days. Three hours and not even a bite. But my partner who fished with me had gone for a wander and found some old, tangled fishing net she brought back to the house with us. She sees beauty in things people miss, one of the reasons I love her. She often brings back wood to use on the fire, rocks to use as kitchen utensils or soap dishes, plastic to throw away, I could go on. That day she saw the beauty in this old relic of roped line, and when I looked at it on the kitchen table, it wasn't just an old net, it was tangled and woven with stories. It now lives in a vase with other bits we've found washed up, like old gripper weights or rigs knotted too tightly for me to want to sit and undo. It also became the inspiration for this book's cover.

A blank can be frustrating. It can really test your patience. Make you want to pack it up for the day earlier than intended. Vexation. If this comes up, something I learned in an IFS (Internal Family Systems therapy) session was to lean into the nervous system's function, instead of trying to reprogramme its already perfect design. Move your body if the frustration builds. Go for a little walk and return. Take your eyes off the rod for a while. Move to a different location if lure fishing or on a boat. Have some lunch. Make notes of tide times, locations or whether it's been overcast or sunny. You might leave empty handed, but maybe you need to empty some.

Catching shouldn't be the only version of success you use as a measurement. Success is a habit that provides a little at a time sometimes. It's not so easily measured in this colonial construct of time. Take the sound of a neighbour learning the saxophone you seem to endure coming through the walls. The same four notes, repeatedly *bah, bam, bum, bah* for weeks. One day you're making a cup of tea and your neighbour is no longer playing four notes, they're playing something. They're playing music. It's always been happening. Just a little at a time.

The wata is teaching us not to be so linear. Take the pics and scroll through them to remind yourself of where you started. Show your date some pics of you fishing if they enquire about this hobby, they will only like you more. Start a social media page and share your journey.

Buy a map or even make a map and plot out where you've fished and what you've caught and, excitedly, where to go next. Talk someone's ear off about top lures versus plastics. Tell the stories over lunch about the fish that was probably a shark, but the line snapped under the weight of this gargantuan creature and, no, you didn't get a pic, you were battling a 20-foot beast!

The success even on a session when you blank is the learning. Consider you now know the sounds of birds that have just seen a shoal and are letting the rest of the crew know. Ok bird whisperer! You know when the tide is coming in just by standing at the shore and feeling its push or pull. Listen, you might just survive that zombie apocalypse, and your friends are right; if World War III does ever happen (it won't), they should come find you because – guess what – you can fish!

Returning

"Mami wata shows up in your dreams."

Fishing has been an opportunity to sit on those riverbanks, that sea, by that river and be back in my own body. Because bodies are made to feel like we belong in them, and mine was not given permission to do so safely until later in life. Our ego is a funny software design: *I made you to protect me* – fair. But after so long the original programme (you) gets othered and pushed to the side so the ego is now always the one in control. Now we're driving through south London at 1am on yet another mission of avoidance, and the original (me), much smaller in the ego's shadow, is in the back seat making suggestions in a small voice, hoping the ego will hear. Nudging and willing us to finally go home.

What is home to you? Certainly, a space, a structure, that covers us. The skin and body we're in that contains us. The family we're born into and the ones we choose. Home can be solid, moving or fleeting. Or all of those things at different times.

Returning home from a fishing session, fresh catch in the cooler or not, is the laying down of work for the day.

Let's start with some practical steps. Building a consistent practice of returning and unpacking keeps your gear organized and protected for future use.

Unpack Your Gear

The best place to start is packing down at the end of a session. A ritual will quickly form according to your own preference, but mine is to try and leave the rods with the line still out, while I pack down chairs and items that are around. I usually then bring in one rod, rest it on the stand, unclip the rig and remove any leftover bait. Before moving on to the next. I always throw unused or unusable bait into the wata but take care to make sure it's just bait – no hooks. I have a few different rods, but all my beach caster spinning rods separate in two or three sections. I pack those down and use Velcro fishing rod straps to hold the pieces together making them easier to travel with. I keep the reel connected to the rod for ease of use the next time. Lastly I pack down the stand. My aim is to have the rods working for as long as possible, just like at the start of a session, when I like to get at least one rod quickly for the same reason.

Clean Your Gear

Now, if you have been fishing in saltwater it's important to rinse your gear with freshwater, as the plastics and metals can be corroded by the salt.

1. Make it a practice at least every third session to use fresh wata, which can be warm with a little soap, and rinse down your reel and rod. As the reel is still connected, it's a simple act of pouring over them. Even if you're fishing in freshwater, weeds and dirt can stick to it so still give it a rinse.

2. Your rigs may have had fresh bait on them, which can become tough if not cleaned. The saltwater will corrode the hook as well. I usually drop my rigs into some warm soapy water once home. If using lures, the hooks will become rusty, so give them a rinse too.

3. If you use a tackle box or a cooler, clean it out well. In the heat of summer if you drop them in the living room, by the next morning, it will smell like Glastonbury on day 4.

Check for Damage

Take this time to give your gear a once over. Look for cracks on the rod and line damage you may have to change before the next session. A classic for me is the quick link leaders I like to use. After a few sessions the link becomes rusty. Without changing them when this happens, you run the risk of it failing when you hook on to anything of a decent size.

Organize and Store

Taking your clean rigs and lures and putting them back into a wallet, foam holder or tackle box will save you having to do a lot of undoing and untangling. It also gives you a visual stamp of how your session went. You get to remember what rigs, hooks, lures worked that day and *how* they worked or how *you* worked *them*.

Reflect

Take your time doing the above steps, if you can. Slow it down. Allow it to be a ritual. Unpacking, checking for damage, organizing. Question whether this is a practice you do for yourself? Have you been taking care of yourself in this way?

It was taught to me by my grandmother, and again by my mother, that gutting fish should happen as soon as possible to preserve the freshness, as you don't want the meat to turn bad – "to spoil". You cannot leave things that will turn bad in the body, can you?

I have been sick. For 10+ years, I was in and out of doctor's appointments complaining of pain in my womb. It was treated like some kind of phantom pain from a removed limb, and I had to swear it was real and plead my case. The year those detectives dressed in plain clothes came to take my statement, was the same year the pain in my womb seemed to grow a consciousness and become fierce, as though disturbed, and annoyed. Tentative doctor's appointments were no longer enough. I had pain one evening that was so bad, I could not keep my eyes open. As much as I willed them to lift, attempting to winch them up with my mind, as my arms lay beside me too heavy and unresponsive to assist, I waited for the ambulance to arrive. As my eyes remained closed and the pain became euphoric and my body became light and weightless, like I was swimming in the ocean, I told myself, no, I don't want to go yet.

Like that, I was pulled back into the bright lights of my bedroom, with people speaking and my cat meowing intensely. Two paramedics appear in my vision and take me to hospital. On arrival, my red blood cell count was 78 and a blood transfusion was immediately administered. That became one of three emergency trips to the hospital and three blood transfusions over six months. The growth in my uterus was for some reason expanding and kicking to be removed, like a child in gestation for far too long.

Eventually it was removed over two operations, and I got my body back. We cannot leave things that will turn bad in the body, can we?

The Mechanism

Fishing can be a mechanism. Reflecting to us the work we have been trying to do unconsciously. The connection to self and others. How the wata calls us on the most random of days. When it might take a car, a train, *and* a bus to get there. So it can remind you to cry salt wata tears too. Or join in on a session with a loved one, even if it doesn't call to you with the same intensity, you get to be with them for a while. A little time you may have needed to spend.

A Reminder of the Work

You may not have received a Master of Optometry degree like the doctors who have dedicated their lives to this, but you have had to interrogate your own eyesight and learned that there are things you can only see in a darkened room when you can laser focus on the parts that call for your attention.

You may not be a trained florist who chooses the perfect combination of colours for the country bouquet that sits like a piece of art, just calling to be photographed and saved for future wedding inspiration, but you've had to learn to make an empty table as beautiful as you possibly can by leaving bouquets to cover the places where the marks were left.

You may not have studied to be a masseuse, but you have had to learn to stretch and release the muscles that have become stiff from the distorted positions you've held over time, as your spirit attempts to fill a shape that was made because of need.

Look at all you are made of. How many lives were there before this present form and iteration of you? How you smile with pride, and nod when people ask, "You fish?" Curious, listening for the why, because every spirit knows the *why* it's done is far more interesting than the *what*. After spending so many hours fishing on those rivers' banks, that sea and a few lakes, I got to thinking about the makings of me too. What have I cast? How long have I waited? And what have I hooked or been hooked to? What did I choose to pack, unpack, knot and undo?

REFLECTION
"My father's house has many rooms."

The first time I felt the power of the wata I nearly drowned in it.

I was on holiday in Jamaica for the first time. The home of my closest known ancestors. I was 21 at the time, exactly half the age I am now. I shouldn't have been there really – holidaying with people I didn't know well enough, trying to keep up with the Joneses of a different rhythm. But I guess not knowing the sway of your own walk at 21 is part of the process.

We were staying in Kingston, the most well-known city of the island – where Bob Marley was from and also the most built-up cosmopolitan part of the island. It's dusty from the always temporary gravel. Whatever was hoped to be concrete and permanent is lifted by heavy rain and the tyres of cars and huge lorries, then mixed with smoke from the food sellers every few feet. It's loud with the sound of motor horns that are used to communicate all things – "I'm behind", "I'm about to go in front", "Move out of my way", "Quick, go in front of me". It's the sound of a people who possess a natural stage–like ability to communicate with one person, but also all the people at the same time. It's a land turned up so high in its natural vibration that it reverberates across the world.

The city of Kingston is inland and because of this has one beach used by locals, Hellshire Beach. Now, all hotels have private beaches, but those are not available for Jamaicans to use freely. Much of the coast in Jamaica, is sold off to these hotels to keep the tourist industry feeling irie and spending money the country needs! So, we (the friend I went with and his immediate family) jumped at the chance to take a trip to Hellshire Beach for the day to cool off from the blazing tropical air that meets your skin immediately and intimately.

The vibe is what you would hope for given the nature of the island – fresh food being cooked up and music from speakers stacked up high playing reggae songs about God, women and weed. I had packed a bikini. I remember this because I went back and forth about what exactly I should be wearing. Women wear bikinis. That was the rule. But that felt so girly. These breasts of mine were already large and buoyant, confirming I was a woman. But I wasn't girly. Womanhood has many forms – I know better now than I knew then. Anyway, I wore the damn thing. That was the rule.

I jumped in the translucent and rippling wata as quickly as I could. A confident swimmer, but this was my first time in the sea. In the UK we would get in waist deep at most while growing up. The seas are rougher, colder and always kind of brown from the rocks and pebbles. But here was different. I was surprised by how I didn't need to kick so hard to stay afloat, like in a pool. The salt content kind of holding me up, a sensation I wasn't prepared for but leaned into immediately. Being held. My body by this age had been wound up tightly for over a decade. To be weightless made me close my eyes automatically and lean my head back and exhale. The warbling sound of the wata as it lapped over my ears was a sweet sensation and, for a moment, I was free without anything to pack or unpack.

Everything changed in an instant. I seemed to now be like one random shoe accidentally added to the washing machine cycle. Bouncing off the edges of the drum, sounding and feeling like chaos and a mistake. I was under the wata and there was no surface. No up or out to aim for. Just under. My eyes were open, but all I could see was bubbles. There was no blue. I tried to activate my arms, but nothing happened. My legs, the same. My limbs had separated from my control, although still attached. For a moment I considered someone was on top of me holding me down under the wata, but I couldn't feel skin, muscles or bones. Unknowingly I was caught in a rip tide.

We are nearing a stage of no more oxygen left in my chest at this point, and the panic had reached a point I have never experienced – post panic. Where nothing happens. No feeling or thought attached. Absolute nothingness. At that moment I was hit by what felt like one of those beeping-car-horn trucks, once and then again. The second wallop and I could sense my arms. My hands are back connected to me and I could feel the solid but smooth surface of rocks. My fingers were gripping like a cat falling down a wall, and I was able to pull my head out of the wata, mouth agape, swallowing as much air as I could before I was pulled under again. There was a level of consciousness to what was happening now, and my soul was back in my body this time, and I said to myself "Not again". Because quite frankly, whatever that was, or is, I wanted off this ride – immediately.

The wave that had taken me under a second time pushed me on top of the rocks, and I found myself seated perfectly as if it were some sort of game and the wata had decided to spit me back out to get a look at me. I'm breathing heavily and deeply and totally unimpressed. Looking to my left and right, I could see I was so far away from where I was earlier floating weightlessly that I could just about make out the group I was with.

When I gathered myself enough and get the oxygen moving through my red blood cells again, I walked back, legs cut up and bruised. The auntie turned to me and said, "Oh you like swimming?"

The next time I felt the power of the wata, I was on tour.

It was about seven years later and the band and I had a show in Reunion Island. We were there for 24 hours, and it took 31 hours to get there. I was 27 at the time and had enough youth in me to think this lifestyle was sustainable. Those rock star years wreaked so much havoc on my body it changed the tone of my voice. But I like it better now anyway. A little weathered and textured.

The show itself was gorgeous. Sunset at the beach with a stage set up just for this event, for those wealthy enough to vacation in such a place.

The morning after the show, knowing we have just a few hours before heading back to the airport for the next leg of the tour, we say "Let's hit the beach". Naturally. The beach in question is L'Hermitage Beach, dreamy and lagoon-like with a coral reef running parallel to the beach, making calm and crystal clear. Our hotel, which led straight onto the beach once you spill from your room, offered canoeing. There were six of us in the crew and there are three two-man canoes available.

We are feeling blessed with the luck we've run into. In one canoe sits Adrian and Dwayne, both Black. There's myself and Laura in the second – I'm Black, she's mixed race – Black and white. In the third canoe sit Kieran and Tom. Kieran is mixed race, white and Black, and Tom is white.

We all kind of focus on our exciting journeys ahead. Adrian and Dwayne set off a little way, and then immediately to the left, rowing adjacent to the beach. I thought Laura and I would do the same, with nowhere ahead of us to aim for but the reef; that made the most sense to me. She's seated in front and I'm behind, as we begin to gently paddle out. The wata is crystal clear, and we can see right to the bottom due its shallowness, only waist deep at its deepest. We're giggling about how we could have brought drinks along with us – not just because of how relaxing this is, but also at that stage in our lives, every occasion was an occasion to have drinks with us.

We hit a little wave and kind of bump over it. Like hitting a road hump while driving at just the right speed. Up and down. It makes us both squeal.

But then we hit another wave and this one feels exponentially larger than the first, causing our canoe to face upward to the sky, and crash back down with a thud. We do not squeal. My antenna sends a message like lightning from the heavens down through my vagus nerve, which is now finely tuned at a constant high vigilance setting, and I say, "OK, let's turn back now". More a pleading than a suggestion.

Her response perplexed me, "We can't turn back now 'cause there is a bigger wave coming and, if we turn now, we'll be sideways and then we'll capsize".

Now Laura and I have been friends for about five years at this point and had drunk at every bar in Soho, and I have never – and I mean never – known her to be a skipper, a captain, an angler or a geologist. So, I say "Nah, we need to turn now", to which she starts to repeat herself "No we can't …". As my ears turn her voice down to let my eyes see better, and I lean to the left to look past her, I get eyes on this wave that is the height of our heads. I dig the paddle down into the wata with the strength of all the those who have lived before me and turn that canoe with such force my shoulder could have dislocated from the socket.

Because I have felt the power of the wata before.

We manage to turn as the wave hits us now from behind and shoves us forward a few feet. Paddling back toward the beach with only the sound of tropical birds squawking and me releasing words the opposite of affirmations in her direction, I can tell from behind, without seeing her face; she is secretly laughing as if it's a good joke at a bad time. Behind my fear and rage, I'm laughing too. As we get back to land and ungracefully exit the canoe as if nothing happened, Adrian and Dwayne are already chilling on the sand.

Dwayne asks us, "Where were you going?"

In our peripheral view while we start to retell the chaos, we all notice one by one like dominoes that Kieran and Toms' canoe is fast approaching that third wave we narrowly escaped. But they are not turning. They hit the wave, and their canoe capsizes sending them both flying in different directions. Kieran is holding onto the reef like tight clothes on a thick body, while Tom is clutching the upturned canoe as the current floats them both out to sea. Immediately, we know they're in trouble, so we start scanning the hotel doors and surrounding area for somebody who can do something. There's no one around. We question if we should, in fact, get in a canoe to save them. Valiant, but not a good idea given our recent voyage. But luckily, we aren't the only people who are watching and a man in a small rib boat is racing toward them. Give tanks.

As he approaches Kieran, who's still hanging on without moving, he too capsizes from the treacherous third wave and is now holding on like glue to the reef that is collecting men like nets collect fish. Tom is still floating out to sea.

Another larger boat starts heading their way, wata kicking up behind it from the power it's using to skate over it. Again, someone is doing something. Our tour crew is in full panic mode at this point and watching helplessly as the wata does whatever it wants with our people. This larger boat manages to feed itself over that third wave, using timing and power adjustments, and collects all three people safely.

Kieran steps off the boat first. He's wearing a string vest that day, but not now –it looks like a string vest onesie as his whole body is covered in small cuts. It turns out that reefs are extremely sharp, which is why he couldn't move an inch while stuck on it. Tom steps off next, and he is white as a ghost. It's the first time I recognized that saying to be true.

We sat there on the beach for a while. Stunned. Amused. Thankful.

I didn't think about that story or its deeper meaning much at all until I started writing this book nearly two decades later.

If Today Was the Last Time I Fished

There are moments, rod in hand and bent at the tip, feeling the shakes and pulls, when you have no time to waste on dissecting motives or wasting precious brain power rehearsing what you should have said or will say if given the chance again. The whole body is engaged, eyes wide taking in all the current data. The muscles in your cheeks are pulling the corners of your lips so high it feels like they are connected to imaginary string. In those minutes, you are completely unashamed of wanting something and feeling deserving of it. I know I am.

We're learning through fishing that there are sandbars, currents, trenches, wrecks and reefs. We're exploring not just how to fish but how the wata changes its surroundings or chooses to move around obstacles. We're realizing that even when it seems calm on the surface, there's likely an undercurrent that can pull us to places unprepared. We're rediscovering with an innate reverence for its power as well as what's in it. We're catching food that will nourish us, while recognizing we must sometimes return the catch to let it grow. This way of life won't save the world but keeps us a part of it. It's a skill to be proud of.

I am proud of this skill and the healing it has provided, but let me be clear, it's been no kind of get-rich-quick scheme into wholeness. It did not untangle a lifetime of me believing I am safest when alone, because love and attention were taught to me as transactional as I learned I had to give away parts of myself without consent to receive anything in return. Even those closest to us, who should care and protect us, come with hidden teeth like a predator species. It's like the ritual of untangling fishing rigs after each session – I'm still undoing all this, stuff.

It did not stop me side-eying kindness for its hidden grenades or meant I didn't scream into my pillow so the neighbours wouldn't hear the grief escape me the day I understood that no one could have saved me, and no one is coming to do so now, because I am the only one who is meant to. It may be a little bit of saving over a lifetime of trying, and knowing that makes me sad for how tired I must be.

But I can feel the vibrational edges of my ego breaking down as the vulnerability pushes through, like the wata nearly transporting me into another lifetime that day in Jamaica. So, speaking to what I want to catch and who or what I want to be caught by, and who must be held wholly responsible for such an unholy catch, is breaking cycles that were generations is the making.

Yes, my body still holds memories that I must stretch and dance out, because letting the energy move, just like the wata does, is what a body was made to do. And the consequence of not doing so quietens it until it is literally stagnant – like swamp wata without flow so filled with the deadliest kind of catches. So even when I come to fish sometimes, I dip my hands in the wata as an act of baptism and ask it to teach me again.

Fishing did not heal all my wounds and erase my past because it was never meant to. Its purpose was to give me reason to show up as my messy and guarded self, and still be allowed to be a part of something bigger. Fishing, for me, became a practice in not feeling so alone in an act of saving myself.

a front door opens to a vinyl runway mat along the length of the hallway. On a Saturday this place sounds of reggae music and a hoover doing its duty earlier than a growing and forming body would choose, if the choice was theirs. This place smells like flavours layered in perfect amounts of complementary spices, passed down over generations like a badge of honour saying, "You will be here, after me, so take this with you." Alongside the mat there are shoes just stepped out of, in neat row. Because in this house, no shoes are to be worn – a separation from what's out there and what is in here. At the end of the hallway there's a table for the house keys to be placed on daily on one's return, with a mirror hanging above it. It's watching for who enters like ancestors keeping an eye out for clean hearts and warm hands. Next to the keys is a rotary phone that swings from right to left in a circular motion as it registers each number, making a phone call something more like a ritual than a mistake.

just like approaching the wata's edge where the local fishermen and fisherwoman rest at half mast, as if their day is half complete and everyone else's is just beginning. Cars containing locals in the know come here because this is where to get the catch of the day and entertaining conversations that are a chorus of three people speaking at the same time, stacked together like chords. You can hear each one though, if you tune in to the right frequency. The cars are parked alongside each other on the gravel made by years of drivers choosing that spot, like a path made through grass people use right next to a concrete version laid especially for them by those who couldn't have known that it was not the path that made most sense. Each car has just enough room for everyone to get in and out if you're skilled enough. It smells like salt and fossils compressed over centuries here and sounds like the Earth breathing.

to the left of the hallway is a living room. There are children here, friends of the families who are chosen through the soul's attraction, as well as those by relation, such as cousins and second cousins and third cousins, who are simply called cousins for ease and respect. In this little world they've created in this living room, there is a TV with static you can feel and a couch that is large enough to become a walkway for when the floor is lava.

just like the coastal bays that are home to small fish that are still growing, or those fully grown, but nature has decided were meant to stay this size to protect the natural order. This bay is a nursery for spawning fish as it's perfectly protected by the shallows that are rich in food sources to support growth and create safety in numbers for those that use it.

In this home, my home, where adults of at least two generations compare how their expectations were not quite met but knew it would be so without having to explain how, understood each other with a look or a nod. They speak strength into one another like witches at a coven casting spells for themselves and others. Where they share plates of food lovingly by talented hands, in a system designed for them to hardly ever get enough time, to look deeply at the lines and read their own fortunes.

In this home, my home, my home, I believed and said aloud with all of my chest, for many decades, was a broken one. But if today was the last day I fished, I'd know that wata cannot break. It can only rise and fall each day revealing piece by piece more of ourselves and where we can flow, and flowed from. It is a slow process happening a little at a time – far better than all at once when it would quite simply take our breath away. What is happening under the surface can seem to happen silently, away from view, but history tells us it can create a sound loud enough to echo across the globe when it needs to.

Like the wata, we can be treated as a forgotten place while judged for desiring to be seen while we continue to carry the stories of our kin and community.

The Story of an Orca Flying a Spaceship

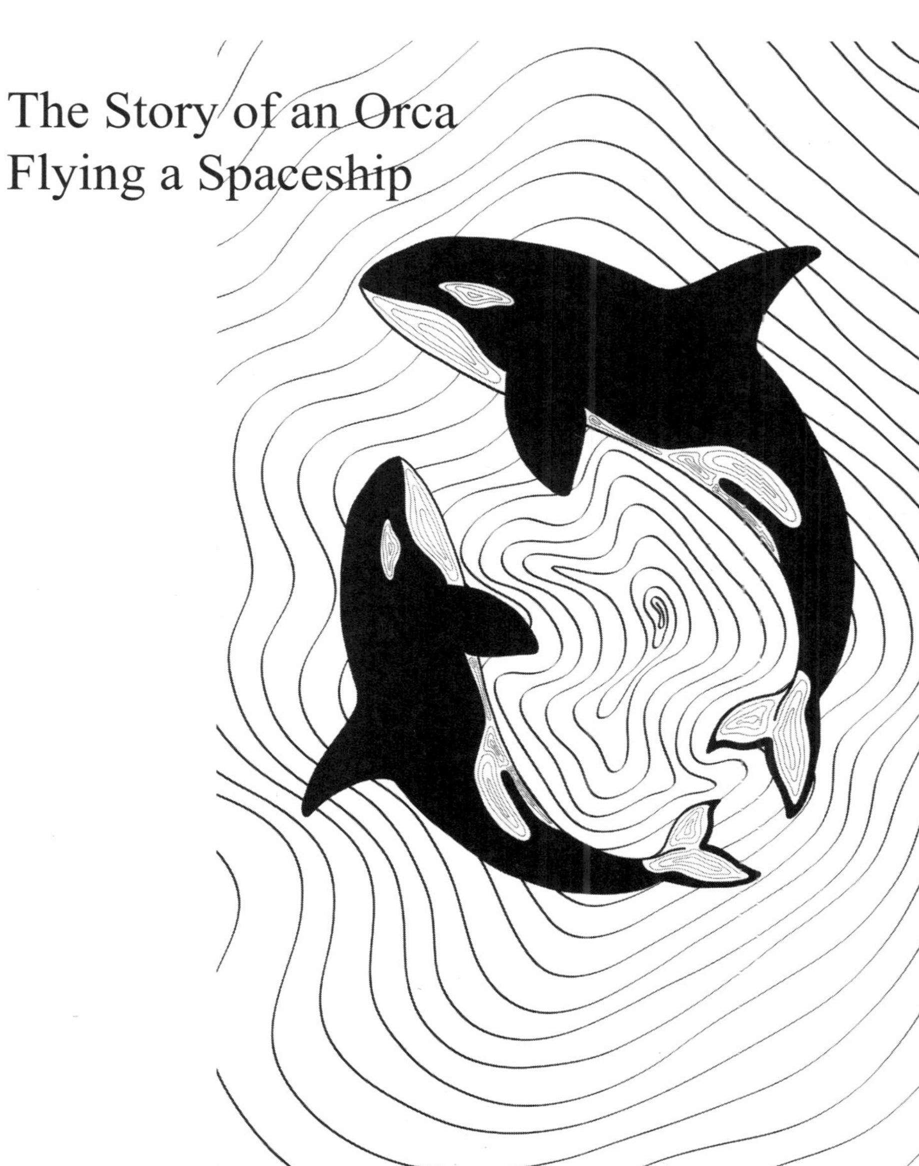

"The orcas are attacking boats and they don't know why."

In May of 2020, the world noticed a strange set of behaviours in a family of orcas. Led by an orca dubbed Gladis Blanca and for reasons unknown, they started attacking boats, yachts and fishing vessels in an area nicknamed the Orca Valley in the Iberian peninsula, along the coast of Portugal and Spain. A once harmonious pod, over the course of five years they attacked at least 250 vessels and sank eight, leaving the world baffled. What was noticeable was that the attacks specifically targeted the vessels' rudders, which are the mechanism that controls a boat's direction by moving from side to side, deflecting the flow of wata, and thus changing the boat's trajectory.

Blanca had come to know the significance of a rudder, having witnessed first-hand the capturing of one the young orcas in her pod decades before, from an area near Iceland during one of their migrations to their home, which is now in Portugal. She remembered in the cells of her body the series of loud and echoing explosions in repetition that reverberated through her skin, causing the clicks of their mothers, trying in vain to communicate to the young to follow, to be disturbed. She remembered the small eyes of the captors, afraid and jittery as though they themselves did not know how they found themselves here, doing this. But for some reason, in laser sharp detail, she remembered that – as the vessel circled them, in a way she had never witnessed anything move before, slowly and incrementally, but somehow also propelled by a great force – the movement was controlled by this rudder. In spite of all that occurred that day, this mechanism would later become important.

As time passed after the theft of her kin all those years ago, the delicate balance they had attempted to recapture was becoming increasingly upended by vessels that seemed to multiply in ways nature could not keep up with nor did not formulate. The vessels were not only here for the capture of orcas, but for species of all kinds. In their pursuit of a food source, the humans were destroying all in their path as they saw the ocean as a soulless space rather than a sacred home A space they wanted to dominate and own. As their fishing vessels and trawlers scoured the sea, ripping apart its fabric, other orcas would often be maimed and unable to make the migration needed to sustain them. Additionally, the vessels caused the numbers of fish for them to feed on to dwindle, creating a knock-on effect in the ocean's ecology. Unhealthy, injured and hungry, the pods were becoming smaller and smaller as each generation of pods were born.

So, one day in the year 2020, in the season of the sea's great green abundance, Blanca executed a plan she had formulated on one of their long migrations. Along with her two sisters, they were to attack a vessel and leave it incapable of moving, sending a message to the humans that the guardians of the sea had spoken. Gladis Blanca, Gladis Dalila and Gladis Clara carried out their attack. Approaching from the stern, stealthily so as not to be seen or heard, Dalila and Clara moved to each side of the boat, while Blanca remained at the stern where the rudder was positioned. Dalila rammed the boat from the port side causing it to nearly spin in a complete circle. From the starboard side, Clara thrashed her tail into the side of the boat, as the humans ran from one edge to another while the boat rocked, dipping its edges nearly entirely into the wata. The men on board tried to anchor themselves to whatever was secularly attached and even each other, as they tried in vain to get eyes on what was happening. Meanwhile, with all the strength Blanca could muster, she grabbed the rudder with her teeth and tore it off completely.

After only a few minutes the orcas could see that without its rudder, this obnoxiously loud structure was no longer heaving through the wata, but limp and floating aimlessly. It had worked. The pod flipped into the air and spouted wata from their blowholes over the vessel in an act of bravado for their strength and their well-executed plan. A warning, for humans not to come back here and just take what they wanted. The Orcas revelled in their first victory and set out to continue these attacks until the message was received and responded to accordingly.

Stories of the orcas' attacks spread like wildfire amongst the humans, sparking conversations about the *mental health* of the orcas, as though they had been invaded by some kind of virus that contorted their behaviour into something strange and alien. Others pleaded at the shores and outside of government buildings that this must be a direct reaction to the health of the oceans and how human life has impacted it.

But the same systems that marginalized the humans and the orcas alike continued to prioritize industrial interest. While the orcas were calling for a reckoning and demanding recognition of the interconnectedness of all life in the only language they shared with humans, the response from authorities seemed non-existent, imagining this all away. It could not just be the need for fish that fuelled their ignorance, but perhaps admitting responsibility for the destruction they had caused would be the unravelling of the fragile structure they themselves had created. Would they lose the power they have over the people if they told the people the truth?

For the next five years, the orcas waged that same style of war on any vessels they deemed a target. Each time they would discuss their findings with Blanca. Some of the orcas felt it was important not to attack smaller and local vessels, a kind of *code of honour* among the guardians. Others believed with a fierceness that *by any means necessary* they must stop the destruction of the ocean, meaning all boats and vessels should be attacked and sunk. Factions emerged within the initial pod and its comrades from surrounding pods who had joined the revolt. Some wanted to carry out these attacks in new areas where the screams of the fish could be heard along with the screams of the people – people who yearned to enter the wata for its healing properties and to eat just like the orcas did, but because of war on land were banished from entering or fishing it.

"How can we save ourselves here in the ocean without saving those on land too?" One of the orcas questioned pleadingly.

The task of these orcas to redress balance was becoming greater than they had expected. This was not just an orca and fish issue. It was a wata issue, which meant it was an Earth issue. But Gladis believed that right here, on the peninsula off the coast of Spain, is where the fight began, and where the fight would end. Eventually, they made an agreement that instead of sinking any boats, they would continue to only destroy the boats' ability to move. If they could not move, they could not steal, was the belief. This was not always possible though, with between eight and 150 boats being completely sunk – casualties of war, they concluded.

But the vessels kept on coming. As one was damaged, another seemed to take its place. Faster than the orcas could respond, these intruders continued to strip the ocean of its bounty with an insatiable hunger. To make matters worse, on one of their official post-attack gatherings, one of the orcas shared a rumour that the people had been laughing at the attacks all along. Apparently, a large gathering of scientists watched footage taken and investigated data collected from previous attacks, concluding that it was nothing more than an act of playfulness by the orcas – some kind of cultural behaviour being displayed. Strange, yes, but nothing more than what was expected from a "lesser species".

The pod erupted at being unseen for their act of resistance – minimized to an act of play as though it did not take grit, intelligence and community gathering to execute such perfectly executed attacks. As though, they, the keepers of the wata, were not formidable. The orcas cried into the vast wata in unison, a call they did not know they knew or had the power to make, joining generations before them with a song that lived in their deepest memories.

"This will be a revolution," screamed Blanca. "We are not mere creatures of instinct, only two-thirds whole, but entirely complete and here – and alive!" The orcas clicked and whistled as the energy from the pod called in other pods feeling the same, understanding they were needed now, because something was about to change. But the call created a change none had expected, as some kind of symbiosis began happening in the wata surrounding them. The marine plants like algae and kelp bent at their holdfast, creating geometric patterns on the seafloor. The fish once hidden and out of sight in between the plants were now exposed. But instead of fearing becoming prey, they started to swim along the routes created by the plants, as though racing around newly created currents, around and around these whirlpools like they were driven by some unspoken mission. Each succession of laps, more fish joined, focused and swimming faster and faster.

The orcas flipped their tails in quick succession humans' hands hitting the skin of drums in unison in an Ifa ceremony. Creating vibrations that called in the reptiles, such as turtles, and invertebrates like squid and crab.

Gladis shouted, "We are guardians of the sea, our existence means something, and we must be heard," as the orcas continued, this uproar now becoming larger with even more pods approaching, more fish, more octopus, more dolphins, more everything.

The birds lifted from their resting places along the coastline and headed in the direction of the orcas' call. Local fishermen who would have previously seen this as an indication of a great day's catch, froze, stunned into silence, their bodies unable to function other than to tilt heads and slowly anchor their necks as their eyes followed hundreds of thousands of birds moving across the sky above them.

Sensors placed in the open ocean by scientists started detecting strange anomalies. Sudden changes in the wata flow and temperature sent alarm signals to their computers, which showed graph lines that instead of steadily moving across the screen, looked like graffiti painted erratically. Calls from scientists to their governments and from those governments to international governments were made. Fighter jets were deployed to the peninsular to get a visual on what exactly was causing the wata to erupt in this way.

People in their homes and work started to lose signal due to the cables that sit along the seabed being broken and disconnected in the melee. This did not stop the news from spreading quickly though, as videos from holidaymakers showing the wata on the beach were uploaded and watched by millions within hours. Or through the fishermen who had made their way back to land to report that "all of the birds are moving". Like a secret meant to be kept, it moved with a quickness across the islands.

Now, whether intentionally or not, this enactment from the orcas and other species had begun to open a portal from the sea floor to the space below. Below the black.

By the time the jets had arrived, all that was left was the aftermath of a revolution, like bits of paper and Coke cans and random shoes left in the street after a human revolution. They circled the area but could not go into the depths.

For weeks on land, the humans debated online about the tsunami that did not happen, the hurricane that did not blow any wind: "The birds man says the birds don't just fly like that for nothing". But the conspiracies changed trajectory immediately, when on 25 September 2025, governments revealed that an object had been seen by a submersible camera right at the edge of the camera's range of focus and ability capture images – an object that had not been seen in anyone's lifetime. It seemed to move from one spot to another at a significantly higher speed than anything they had ever seen before. It was much larger than it should be based on its speed, and it appeared to be made of nickel and iron, with a chemical profile not documented on any living organism. They named this craft-type vessel the Assatta 3I.

For six months the people watched Assattta 3I whenever it appeared, just enough to be noticed but not enough to be truly seen, as it popped up from coast to coast across the planet. In line with the Assatta's appearances, fewer and fewer orca attacks occurred. In fact, less of anything seemed to occur in the wata. Trawlers that normally collected tons of fish at a time were coming back with smaller and smaller numbers. Boats trips to watch the sunset on catamarans said the flying fish, so loved by the customers for their magic show of jumping across the waves, had not been spotted.

On 21 April 2026, Assatta 3I showed itself for the last time and with it, the last species to inhabit the wata was ever seen. It was as though the craft had collected them and taken them into a different space altogether, where they could be free and their songs could resonate without interruption, with the weight of oppression lifted. All that remained were small holes in the sea floor that let a kind of light shine through the darkness and twinkle in the wata's current. A reminder of a world that once was.

This story is inspired by true events that started in May 2020. A group of orcas started attacking boats, yachts and fishing vessels in an area nicknamed the Orca Valley, in the Iberian Peninsula along the coast of Portugal and Spain.

The name Gladis was given by the marine biologist who first identified the group of Orcas. It is a reference to the old scientific name for orcas, *Orcinus Gladiator*, which means "whale-fighter" in Latin.

The orcas were, and still are, attacking boats, yachts and fishing vessels and the scientist cannot decide why.

Acknowledgements

Crystal Mahey-Morgan, Ella Chappell, Alexis Lee, Ana Pryor, Mercy Thokozane Minah and Dr Leighan Renaud

you have all been the inspiration and support needed to bring this book into fuition and I am truly, truly grateful.